The Motor-Cyclists Handbook 1911

By
'Phoenix'

Originally Published by Percival Marshall & Co

Reprinted by Classicmotorcyclemanuals.com

Published by
classicmotorcyclemanuals.com 2012

Stephen Brown January 2012

ISBN 978-1-908890-00-9

Printed by the MPG Books Group Bodmin and King's Lynn

Introduction

Having been introduced to the joys of motorcycling at age 13 by various off road exploits on numerous Lambretta Scooters, BSA, Dandy's and NSU Quickly's. I soon became hooked, taking a job as a telegram lad and living every day for my motorcycling on a series of BSA, Triumph, Ariel, AJS, Matchless and Velocette motorcycles. One way and another all this and much more eventually led me to republish this book.

Moving swiftly on by 40 years, I present Phoenix, a young enthusiastic motorcycle engineer who wrote The Motor Cyclists Handbook 100 years ago and amazed me by his knowledge and skill in writing and illustrating this book. It is an absolute gem for the Vintage Biker.

I dedicate this book to my mother Margaret who put up with the Ariel under my bed, my father Cyril who was my guru on all old bike matters and my friends Jimmy Middleton, Capt. Ian Ives and John Collins who have enriched so many lives by their sheer enthusiasm for Vintage and Classic motorcycles. Finally, a tribute to my friend Gordon May who continues to astound me by undertaking very long motorcycle journeys on some very old motorcycles. I hope you enjoy the book.

M—R

THE LEADING LIGHT WEIGHT MOTOR CYCLE

The M.R. Models represent the first and last steps in motor-cycling. If you are a beginner or one with modest requirements the 2 h.-p. Single Cylinder will suit you admirably.

If you are rather more expert and ambitious, or wish to own a better machine than you are at present riding, you will find the $2\frac{3}{4}$ h.-p. Twin the very Motor Cycle *de luxe*. <u>Both models are extremely reliable, economical, simple, and light, and perfectly weather-proof.</u>

Send for Catalogue Free.

Moto-Reve Co. Ld. Dept. T. Acton Vale, London, W.

S & H

BURBERRY
MOTOR CYCLE OUTRIG

Designed to meet the views of an expert Motor Cyclist, well acquainted with all needs and the most practical methods of satisfying them.

The Jacket is double-breasted, with Pattee collar, buttons over and under completely across the chest.

Long pull-overs, coming almost up to the armpits, form a further covering and protect the legs and thighs against wet, mud and dust.

GABARDINE

The material used for this outfit is woven and weatherproofed by special Burberry processes; it excludes rain, wind and cold, is naturally ventilating and of incalculable durability. It is further fortified by a lining of wool or camel-fleece, which unites the maximum warmth and comfort with the minimum weight.

WRITE FOR BROCHURE V.
BURBERRY FOR MOTOR CYCLING.

BURBERRY'S, 30, 31 & 33, Haymarket, LONDON.
10, Boul.-Malesherbes, PARIS.

Basingstoke and Appointed Agents in Chief Provincial Towns.

We are Motor Cycle Specialists.   We have the Largest Stocks.

WE EQUIP THE MOTOR CYCLE WORLD

WITH ACCESSORIES AND CLOTHING   AND SUPPLY EVERY MAKE OF MOTOR CYCLE

THE
SERVICE
Co. Ld. FOR MOTOR CYCLES

We hold the largest actual stock of new and second-hand machines of every size, weight and power, and are Agents for every well-known make, including :—

WANDERER, TRIUMPH, HUMBER, REX, INDIAN, MOTO-RÊVE, KERRY-ABINGDON, F.N., PREMIER, ARIEL, DOUGLAS, ENFIELD, BRADBURY, DOT MATCHLESS, & MILLFORD SIDE CARS, Etc., Etc

We sell for Cash, Gradual Payments, or Exchange. Your old machine taken in part payment. Any machine advertised in this book can be best purchased through us. Write or call and inspect our Showrooms.

LOWEST PRICES — QUICKEST DELIVERY

Send for complete Catalogue of Machines, Accessories, and Clothing. Post Free. The largest issued in the Trade.

292 - 3 HIGH HOLBORN, LONDON, W.C.

Telegrams: "Admittedly, London."   Telephone: 260 Central.

THERE is no part of a Motor Cycle Engine so insignificant that it does not require to be properly designed.

Probably more care and thought have been expended upon the design of the famous

SPARKING PLUG

than on any other cycle accessory.

The Lodge Plug is suitable for *all* Motor Cycles, and the price is only

4/-

If not already using it, try one on your engine at once. You will never regret it. It is fully guaranteed.

A steel gauge, push-on terminal, and copper-asbestos washer, free in box with every plug.

When ordering, specify "Motor Cycle" type.

Can be obtained from all the best dealers, or post free, by return (when remittance accompanies order), direct from the makers:—

LODGE BROS. & Co.

Dept. Q., New Street,

BIRMINGHAM.

3 POINT SPARK GAP.

DUNHILL'S MOTORITIES
FOR MOTOR CYCLISTS.

ALL THAT IS BEST IN MOTOR CYCLING CLOTHING AND ACCESSORIES.

THE RIGHT GOODS AT THE RIGHT PRICES.

Dunhill's Acetylene Motor Cycle Lamp, Lens Mirror, Adjustable Focus, 18/6.

Write now for your copy of our

CATALOGUE,

which, amongst its 56 pages and 300 Illustrations, includes all the necessary Accessories and Clothing needful to the up-to-date Motor Cyclist.

Motor Cycle Exhaust Whistle, in solid brass. Suitable for one or two cylinder machines. **7/6.** This whistle, being of solid brass throughout, has a more mellow note than any other Motor Cycle Exhaust Whistle on the market.

Trouser Overalls, in double texture waterproof, 13/6, 16/6, and 21/-.

In Dunwear, lined camel, 30/-.

DUNHILL'S
359-361, Euston Road, LONDON, N.W.

88, Cross Street, MANCHESTER.

72, St. Vincent Street, GLASGOW.

FOR...

MOTOR CYCLES, &c.

TRY...

Holborn Autochange Ltd.

100, HIGH HOLBORN,
Telephone 3910 CITY.   LONDON, W.C.

WHO ARE NOTED FOR RELIABLE MACHINES AND FAIR TREATMENT.

MOTORS BOUGHT AND SOLD.   REPAIRS. ACCESSORIES.

"AMAC"

CARBURETTORS,
BELT PUNCH,
BELT FASTENER,
MAGNETO CONTROL,
FILLER CAP,
COMPRESSION COCK,
PETROL COCK,
TERMINAL CLIPS,
HANDLE BAR
        SWITCHES.

ASTON MOTOR ACCESSORIES CO., LTD.
Talford Street, Aston,
            BIRMINGHAM.

THE "CLAIR" SILENCER
(PATENT).
The Scientific Method of dealing with EXHAUST GASES.

NO FLAT SURFACES.
NO ASBESTOS.
NO SOOTING.
NO PIERCED PIPES.

NO BALLS OR CORRUGATED PARTS.
NO RIVETS.
STRONGLY MADE.

99% Efficiency.   Fit any Cycle.   British Made.
MORE POWER—GREATER SILENCE.

SOLE MANUFACTURERS—

J. C. LYELL & Co, Ltd.,

Telephone: 2469 GERRARD.   Telegrams: "ELECTRINUS," LONDON.   113, Great Portland Street, LONDON, W.

"IVY PRECISION" 3¾ h.-p. (Ball Bearing Engine).

£40   S. A. NEWMAN,   £40

Enquiries Solicited.
Art Catalogues post free.

IVY CYCLE WORKS,
LICHFIELD ROAD, BIRMINGHAM.
Telephone: 321 East.

The 'HANDY HOBART'

BROOKLANDS 100 MILES RECORD
For Light-weight Motor-cycles, is held by Mr. A. Webster, on his "Handy Hobart."

The Leading and Best Light-weight.

2¾ h.p. Model, Bosch Magneto, Drip-feed Lubrication, Druid Spring Forks, Adjustable Aluminium Footrests, New "Hobart" Heel-applied Belt Rim Brake, Handle-bar Controls. Weight, 108 lbs., exact.

Price = = = = = = £38
SPEED FROM 4 TO 40 MILES PER HOUR

3½ h.p. Twin Cylinder.—Latest Design.

Bosch Magneto, Drip-feed Lubrication, Druid Spring Forks Adjustable Aluminium Foot-rests, "Hobart" Belt Rim Brake, Clincher or Dunlop Tyres, Handle-bar Controls. Weight, 150 lbs. (approximate.)

Price - = = = - - 47 Guineas.

Catalogue and full particulars gladly sent on request.

HOBART BIRD & Co., Ltd., Dept. T9, COVENTRY.

Owners are satisfied.

N.S.U. Motor Cycles owe their popularity to the fact that they are always abreast of the times in structural and mechanical improvements. Moreover, they have a firm reputation for thorough reliability, easiness of control, power on hills, and unrivalled economy.

1911 MODELS.

2 h.p. Single cylinder, 66 × 78 m/m. Mechanical Valves, Spring Forks and Spring Frame.

3 h.p. Twin cylinder, 58 × 75 m/m. With Spring Forks and Spring Frame.

The above are entirely new models.

1½ h.p. Light weight, Single cylinder, 63 × 78 m/m.
2¾ h.p. Do. Twin cylinder, 52 × 74 m/m.
3½ h.p. Standard Touring, Single cylinder, 85 × 88 m/m.
6 h.p. Standard Touring, Twin cylinder, 75 × 90 m/m.

Some of the chief features :—New Spring Forks ; New Spring Frame ; New Cable Brake ; New Stand ; Adjustable Pulley ; Two-Speed Gear and Free Engine ; New N.S.U. Carburettor ; Loop Frame.

N.S.U. MOTOR Co., Ltd.

Offices and Showrooms—
186, Gt. Portland St., LONDON, W.

Goods and Repairs—
83-85, Bolsover St., LONDON, W.

TO THE MOTOR CYCLIST.

Accessories that are indispensable.
TO SHOW YOUR SPEED AND MILEAGE.

THE
'JONES' Speedometer
STEADY AS A ROCK.

Accurate as the Greenwich Time Ball.

Unapproachable for
RELIABILITY, ACCURACY,
AND GOOD SERVICE. . .

MODELS:

26. Speed to 60 or 80 m.p.h., and Season's Mileage to 10,000 miles **£3 3 0**
31. Includes also trip mileage and automatic reset **£4 4 0**
32. Above with addition of maximum speed hand **£5 5 0**

TO SHOW YOUR MILEAGE (Trip and Season's Total) use the

"VEEDER."

It enables you to gauge—

The wear of the machine and its parts — petrol consumption per mileage — tyre records, and for measuring daily trips and season run.

SUPPLIED TO SUIT DIFFERENT SIZE WHEELS.

PRICE 12/6.

FULL PARTICULARS OF

MARKT & Co. (London), Ltd., 6, CITY ROAD, LONDON, E.C.

BUILD YOUR OWN MOTOR CYCLE

We supply Sets of Castings, Forgings, &c., complete with Blue Prints.

Sets of Lugs to build Frames, or Complete Frames.

LIST FREE ON APPLICATION.

ALFRED NOBLE & Co., Hill St., COVENTRY,

Manufacturers and Factors of Engines, Frames, Carburettors, Magnetos, Wheels, Tyres, Hubs, Free Engine Devices, Speed Gears, &c., &c.

Lest You Forget!

The Best and Cheapest House for anything Motor-cyclish,

NEW, SHOP-SOILED, SECOND-HAND, OR BANKRUPT STOCK,

—— IS ——

C. H. HITCHEN'S,

The Lancashire Motor Exchange,

EUSTON ROAD, MORECAMBE.

My stock of New and Second-hand **MOTOR CYCLES** and **SIDE CARS** is always bigger than any other house.

MY TERMS ARE CASH, DEFERRED, or EXCHANGE.

I am always ready to swap, chop and change. I want to Buy for cash what you want to Sell, and to Sell what you want to Buy. You cannot do better, and you may easily do worse.

WRITE ME AT ONCE FOR MONTHLY LIST.
It is awaiting your Post Card.

The Frontispiece of this Volume

Shows the Author, "PHŒNIX," with his $2\frac{3}{4}$-3 h.-p. medium weight "ARNO" MOTOR BICYCLE, of which he writes as follows :—

Messrs. The Arno Motor Co., Ltd.,
    Coventry.
                                                    London, E.C.
                                                    Jan. 20th, 1911.

Dear Sirs,—The $2\frac{3}{4}$-3 h.p. medium weight "Arno" Motor Bicycle, which I purchased from you early last autumn, is proving satisfactory in every way. The engine is a marvel of flexibility, and its power capacity far exceeds my anticipations. It will fire regularly at astonishingly low speeds, and the machine has shown itself capable of reaching 50 m.p.h. by speedometer on the level road. I am more than satisfied with its hill-climbing qualities, while it is very economical both in petrol consumption and tyres. Other good points are the ready accessibility of the engine and other parts, and speaking generally, I am extremely pleased with the machine as a whole.   Yours faithfully, "PHŒNIX."

This is the Machine referred to in the above Letter.

$2\frac{3}{4}$-3 h.-p. "ARNO."

It has a BALL-BEARING ENGINE, STRONG FRAME (Registered Design), DRUID SPRING FORKS H.B.C. CARBURETTOR, PROTECTED MAGNETO, comfortable RIDING POSITION, with FOOTBOARDS, and very smart appearance. The ENTIRE POWER UNIT is DETACHED BY SIMPLY REMOVING FOUR VERTICAL BOLTS. We also manufacture a more POWERFUL MODEL with $3\frac{1}{2}$-4 H.-P. ENGINE, and rather heavier Construction throughout.

For ECONOMY, SIMPLICITY, RELIABILITY and SPEED with COMFORT Ride ARNO MOTOR BICYCLES manufactured THROUGHOUT at the

Arno Motor Works
GOSFORD STREET, COVENTRY, ENG.

SPHINX IGNITION PLUGS

Will make your Motor Spin like a Top.

Because they are made in a factory equipped for the one purpose only — the largest of its kind in the Kingdom.

HENCE it follows that every workman not only thoroughly understands his work, but also the object of it.

The Result is the production of sound, lasting, and fully guaranteed Plugs, which may be relied upon under all conditions.

These Plugs, packed in decorated green tin boxes with red seals, may be obtained of all Agents and Garages.

Best in 1904 and Best to-day.   British Manufacture.

Full Illustrated Price List sent on request to—

The SPHINX MANUFACTURING Co.
242, Bradford Street, BIRMINGHAM.

To buy the Best is to buy a Triumph.

Aud the Best is always the Cheapest in the end.
You will find this so with a

TRIUMPH
MOTOR CYCLE

There is nothing equal to it for the trustworthy service it will render—its small repairs bill, and its economical fuel consumption, and then when you have finished with it, it will command a ready sale and realise a good price as a second-hand.

The Triumph Motor Cycle is the original of its type, it has proved its reliability in the hands of thousands of present-day riders. Do not experiment—it costs money—but choose a Triumph and you choose well.

**THE TRIUMPH FULLY DESCRIPTIVE CATA-
LOGUE IS AT YOUR DISPOSAL, POST FREE.**

Triumph Cycle Co., Ld., Coventry.

London: 4 5, Holborn Viaduct, E.C.   Glasgow: 101, Mitchell St.
Manchester: 160, Deansgate.   Leeds: 4, King Edward St.

THE MOTOR CYCLIST'S HANDBOOK.

The Author ("Phœnix")
with 3-h.p. "Arno" Motor Bicycle.

THE
MOTOR CYCLIST'S HANDBOOK

A Practical Manual on the Construction
and Management of Motor Cycles.

By "PHŒNIX"
(Chas. S. Lake. A.M.I.Mech.E.).

FULLY ILLUSTRATED.

LONDON:
PERCIVAL MARSHALL & CO.,
26-29, Poppin's Court, Fleet Street, E.C.

CONTENTS.

CHAPTER		PAGE
I.	THE ENGINE: ITS WORKING PRINCIPLE; THE FOUR-STROKE CYCLE; VALVES, AND THE MEANS OF OPERATING THEM	7
II.	THE ENGINE (*continued*): THE TWO-STROKE OR "VALVELESS" SYSTEM	20
III.	TWIN- AND FOUR-CYLINDER MOTOR CYCLE ENGINES (FOUR-STROKE SYSTEM)	30
IV.	CONSTRUCTIONAL DETAILS OF MOTOR CYCLE ENGINES	45
V.	COMPRESSION	60
VI.	THE CARBURETTOR	63
VII.	THE IGNITION	82
VIII.	THE TRANSMISSION: BELT AND CHAIN DRIVES, FREE ENGINE CLUTCHES, AND VARIABLE SPEED GEARS	116
IX.	LUBRICATION	159
X.	THE SPRINGING OF MOTOR CYCLES	165
XI.	OVERHAULING AND TUNING UP THE ENGINE, ETC.	180
XII.	THE MACHINE AS A WHOLE—THE SELECTION AND PURCHASE OF NEW AND SECOND-HAND MACHINES — DRIVING HINTS— PASSENGER MOTOR CYCLES—THE COST OF MOTOR CYCLING	204
XIII.	ACCESSORIES AND EQUIPMENT	242
XIV.	THE LAW IN RELATION TO MOTOR CYCLING	260

PREFACE.

IT has been said, with truth, that an inherent love of things mechanical finds a more or less definite place in the character of every Englishman, even though in many it may be but a latent sense, unassociated either with their business pursuits or pleasures, and there can be little doubt that the motor cycle—which has increased in popularity by leaps and bounds during the past few years—provides a direct and powerful means of fostering that spirit of mechanical aptitude which so many possess without knowing it.

To own a motor cycle is, in effect, to own a private locomotive. capable of transporting its rider up hill and down dale for long distances, with a rapidity impossible with any other class of vehicle of the same size and weight. The delightful sensation of free-wheeling down a long and easy grade on a pedal cycle—an experience which most of us frequently enjoy—is reproduced, with a motor cycle, on the level, up steep hills, and, indeed, in every stage of progress, calling for no effort on the rider's part, and requiring no particular skill in order that the best results may be obtained.

The modern motor cycle is both easy and comfortable to ride and drive ; its construction is relatively simple, and, indeed, every detail connected with its control and maintenance may be completely mastered by anyone of average intelligence in a very short time. In engine power it ranges from the little $1\frac{1}{2}$ h.-p. lightweight to the heavy and powerful 7-9 h.-p. twin-cylinder machine, equipped with two- or even three-speed gear mechanism and suitable for conveying two persons, by means of a side or fore car attachment, from one end of the country to the other, with but very little, if any, difficulty, whatever may be the nature of the hills or the general character of the roads traversed,

Between these two extremes there are to be found many different types of motor cycles, varying in engine-power, price, and constructional details, and, in fact, anyone who, having once made up his mind to become a motor cyclist, and who is prepared to expend a reasonable sum in acquiring a machine suitable to his tastes, need not, now that the motor bicycle has attained its present state of reliability and general efficiency, hesitate for a moment about taking the step which will bring him into personal acquaintance with one of the most delightful pastimes ever introduced.

In the author's experience, however, as contributor of the "Motor Cycle Notes" appearing weekly in the pages of *The Model Engineer and Electrician*, there *does* exist—as is shown by the many inquiries received—a considerable doubt on the part of many as to whether the use and maintenance of a motor cycle does not impose a heavy expenditure in time and money on its owner, and also whether the mechanical ability required in the upkeep of such a machine is not rather in advance of that possessed by the average person. The author's reply to all such queries is a decided negative: for, although it would, of course, be idle to assert that motor cycling is one of the cheapest pastimes, the expenses attending it may, if care be exercised, be kept within quite moderate limits; and while in the early stages of his experience every motor cyclist meets with difficulties which for the moment may appear formidable, the surmounting of these difficulties often provides one of the most interesting and attractive features of the pastime, and fits the rider for tackling any kind of trouble which may subsequently fall to his lot. It is with a view to clearing away such misconceptions as appear to prevail among those who have not yet joined the ranks of the motor cycling community, by placing before them, in as simple and straightforward a manner as possible, the anatomy of the motor bicycle and a description of the functions and formation of its various parts, as well as the uses and capabilities of the machine as a whole, that the preparation of the present work was undertaken—a task, be it known, that owes its conception in some measure to the expressed wishes of many readers of "THE MODEL ENGINEER" Notes.

"PHŒNIX,"

The Motor Cyclist's Handbook.

BY " PHŒNIX."

Contributor of the " Motor Cycle Notes " appearing weekly in *The Model Engineer and Electrician.*

CHAPTER I.

THE ENGINE: ITS WORKING PRINCIPLE; THE FOUR-STROKE CYCLE; VALVES, AND THE MEANS OF OPERATING THEM.

As in every other mechanically driven vehicle, the motorcycle depends for its means of propulsion upon a power unit, which in this case consists of an internal combustion engine consuming petrol gas as its fuel, and working, in the majority of instances, upon the four-stroke, although, in a few recent designs, upon the two-stroke (or double-impulse) principle. The prospective motor cyclist, if he be wise, will first make himself acquainted with the construction and system of working of the engine before setting out to acquire possession of a motor cycle, so that whatever difficulties he may encounter during his novitiate may be the more readily and independently overcome. Subsequent personal experience and acquaintance with the problems that arise, can alone make him a good and efficient driver of a motor cycle, and teach him what he requires to know about the construction and maintenance of the engine and the other parts of his machine.

The Working Principle Explained.

In the four-stroke motor cycle engine, at present the most widely adopted type, a full cycle of operations is completed during two revolutions of the flywheels, commencing with the inlet (or suction) stroke of the piston, which is followed in turn by the compression, working (or explosion), and the final (or exhaust) strokes. When the No. 1 (or suction) stroke takes place, the charge, consisting of a carburetted mixture of petrol and air, is drawn into the cylinder as the piston descends, and is next forced by the following (upward) movement of the latter into the combustion chamber or compression space located in the cylinder head above the travel of the piston, where, owing to the restricted volume, it becomes highly compressed, and is then ready to be exploded with far greater force than would have been possible before compression took place.

FIG. 1.—No. 1, Inlet Stroke.

The ignition of this highly compressed charge is effected by means of an electric spark, timed to occur at a precise moment in relation to the travel of the piston, but at the same time variable within certain defined and narrow limits, as will be explained later in the chapter on Ignition. The resultant explosion acts upon the piston as a propelling force of great magnitude, causing it to descend on the No. 3 (or working) stroke, and thereby rapidly rotate the flywheels—to which latter, as need hardly be added, it communicates motion by means of a connecting-rod.

The next, and final, stroke of the piston impels the exploded gases upwards before it, and the exhaust valve having duly opened just before the completion of the working

FIG. 2.—No. 2, Compression Stroke.

stroke, a way of escape from the cylinder is provided for the burnt, and now useless, gases, which pass out through the exhaust pipe and silencer into the atmosphere. It will thus be seen that of the four separate strokes of the piston which go to make up the complete working cycle of the engine, only one is performed directly under the influence of the explosion, the remaining three being brought about by the momentum which is stored up in the heavy flywheels as the result of the rotative motion communicated to them during the power stroke.

Briefly summarised, then, the four-stroke cycle operates as follows :—

No. 1. The Suction Stroke↓   Charge drawn into cylinder
No. 2. The Compression Stroke↑Charge compressed in cylinder
No. 3. The Working Stroke↓   Charge exploded in cylinder
No. 4. The Exhaust Stroke   ↑Charge expelled from cylinder

FIG. 3.—No. 3, Explosion or Working Stroke.

Reference to the accompanying diagrams (Figs. 1 to 4) will serve to further explain the description given above.

The Action of the Valves.

The inlet and exhaust valves, by means of which the gaseous charge is respectively allowed to enter and leave the cylinder, are generally of the mushroom pattern, as shown in the drawings. The exhaust valve is mechanically operated in every case; that is, it derives its motion from a cam, actuated from the engine main shaft by means of gear, or (as they are usually termed) timing wheels, because they govern, in conjunction with the aforesaid cam, the precise moments at which the valves—for admitting and expelling the gases to and from the cylinder—shall open and close. In the majority of cases where only one cylinder

FIG. 4.—No. 4, Exhaust Stroke.

is employed the inlet valve is also mechanically operated, but some makers prefer to use what are known as automatically-operated inlet valves (for abbreviation, A.O.I.V.), and especially is this so where the engine is of the twin-cylinder type, for reasons which will appear as our description proceeds. Automatic valves depend for their opening upon the partial vacuum created within the cylinder by the descent of the piston on the suction stroke, and such valves being smaller, lighter and cheaper as a whole than mechanical valves; and, further, in view of the fact that they require no timing gear, and can be placed over the exhaust valve instead of needing a separate " pocket " (or chamber) of their own, it is claimed that they simplify the construction and thereby reduce the chances of failure, while another advantage sometimes claimed is that the exhaust valve is effectively cooled by the admission of pure gas immediately above it.

On the other hand, as their opening movement is based upon the action of the piston, and the amount of opening largely depends upon the degree of suction induced by its speed, it will be recognised that the slower the engine runs the less will the valve opening be, so that the area for admission of the gases may be said to vary with the piston speed, and is not necessarily in accordance with the power development required from the engine. A mechanically operated valve has a constant lift at *all* speeds, and possesses the further advantage that it is not dependent to anything like the same extent as the automatic valve upon the strength of its spring for efficient working. It seldom sticks, and with it the engine will run slower and with greater regularity on up grades.

Lack of power in a twin-cylinder motor cycle engine fitted with automatically-operated inlet valves is often traced to a difference in the strength of the inlet valve springs, and even a slight discrepancy is sufficient to affect the running of the engine, as it leads to unequal work being performed in each cylinder, instead of the driving force being equally distributed over the two pistons, as happens when both valves are correctly and uniformly adjusted. Some makers claim that for the highest speeds, and absolute freedom in running, engines equipped with A.O.I. valves are superior to those having M.O.I. valves; but if the matter is to be judged by the relative performances of each type, it must be difficult to substantiate the point.

Automatic inlet valves are undoubtedly much easier to handle than mechanical ones, but they require more constant and skilful attention to maintain them in proper condition.

Recently, certain manufacturers of motor cycles have been fitting their engines with what are termed " overhead " mechanical valves, such valves occupying the same position as A.O.I. valves—*i.e.*, above the exhaust valve chambers, but deriving their motion from the timing gear in the distribution chamber through the medium of long tappet rods, with an overhead rocking lever to allow of a reciprocating vertical motion induced by the action of the cam. Satisfactory results have been achieved with this system, which was first applied to track racing motor cycles and afterwards to the touring models of certain makers; but the author has gathered from users of the valves that in course of working, when the rods and joints have worn somewhat slack, considerable noise is set up, and in many cases the tappet rods have been removed altogether and the inlet valves converted to automatic working. To condemn the use of overhead M.O. valves would, however, be to take an altogether unreasonable view of the matter.

The Timing Gear.

The valve-actuating mechanism, or timing gear, for a mechanically-operated valve consists of two toothed pinions or gear-wheels, one of which is carried by the main shaft of the engine, and the other by what is known as the "half-time," or cam, shaft; this secondary gear-wheel and shaft being, as a rule, formed in one solid piece with the cam itself, and having double the number of teeth on the driving pinion, hence the use of the term "2 to 1" gear. As the engine shaft revolves, the gear-wheel mounted upon it, intermeshing as it does with the cam gear-wheel, revolves the latter at half its own speed and the cam is set at the proper angle to lift the tappet, which in its turn moves the valve (whether inlet or exhaust) at certain prescribed and regular periods in accordance with the movements of the piston and the stage which has been reached in the cycle of operations. Fig. 5 illustrates the timing gear of a single cylinder engine with M.O. inlet and exhaust valves. Matters are so organised that the inlet valve opens just after the piston has commenced the induction stroke to admit the charge into the cylinder, remaining open throughout the length of the suction stroke. Both valves then remain closed during the compression and working strokes, the next valve movement being the opening of the exhaust valve when the piston has reached a point somewhere about $\frac{1}{4}$ in. from the end of the working stroke, followed by its closing again as the exhaust stroke come to an end, and the re-opening of the inlet valve, when, of course, a fresh supply of mixture is needed in order that the cycle may commence over again. Briefly stated, the cycle of movements is as follows :—

(1) Inlet or suction stroke : Inlet valve *open*, exhaust *closed*.
(2) Compression stroke : Both valves *closed*.
(3) Explosion stroke : Both valves *closed*.
(4) Exhaust stroke : Exhaust valve *open*, inlet *closed*.

Fig. 5.—Timing Gear of a Modern Single-cylinder Motor Cycle Engine with M.O. Valves.

The exact setting of the timing gear varies slightly in different engines, but, as a general rule, follows the plan shown in the accompanying diagram (Fig. 6).

It is very important indeed that the timing of the valve movements should be correct, as only a slight error suffices to affect the performance of the engine. When once the correct valve setting has been ascertained in the builders' works, the timing wheels are (or should be) plainly punch

THE ENGINE: FOUR-STROKE SYSTEM. 15

FIG. 6.—Diagram of Valve Setting.

FIG. 7.—The "Triumph" 3½ h.p. Engine, in part Sectional Elevation.

marked or otherwise stamped, so that in the event of its becoming necessary at any subsequent time to disturb the timing, the correct relative positions of the parts may be known and no need will then arise, when reassembling them, to experiment or trouble in any way about the point.

It is customary in well-constructed modern engines to interpose between the cam and the foot of the tappet which

FIG. 8.—Rear End Sectional View of "Triumph" 3½ h.-p. Engine.

lifts the valve a rocking arm or lever, as seen in Fig. 5, which allows of smoother action and results in a wider distribution of the effects of wear on the parts in contact, and so maintains for a much longer period than

THE ENGINE : FOUR-STROKE SYSTEM.   17

otherwise would be the case the desired amount of lift for the valve. Sometimes a roller is used in place of the rocking lever.

Springs for M.O. and A.O. Valves.

In the case of mechanically-operated valves, a lift of about ¼ in. is considered necessary, the point depending to some extent, of course, upon such matters as the bore and stroke of the cylinder, diameter of the valve itself, port areas, and so on ; but automatic inlet valves should never

FIG. 9.—The "Norton" 3½-4 h.-p. Engine.

be allowed more than ⅛-in. opening at the most and, generally speaking, better results will be secured if this is reduced to 3/32 in. The springs employed with inlet and exhaust valves must be correctly proportioned, as regards strength, for the duty they are to perform. Too strong a spring in the case of a mechanically-operated valve throws added resistance on the timing gear, and may in some circumstances result in breakage of the valve itself, due to its head being brought down on to the seating with undue force. On the other hand, too *weak* a spring, or one that has lost its life and temper as a result of long service and the effects of being heated up so frequently, makes the engine sluggish in running, and liable to overheat. It is necessary that the valves should both open and close smartly (apart from the time they remain open), and that there shall be a free and

FIG. 10.—Peugeot Motor Cycle Engine with Single Cam for Actuating two M.O. Valves.

uninterrupted circulation of the gases through the cylinder during the periods of induction and exhaust, and, of course, the *amount* of opening is a matter of paramount importance.

Automatic inlet valve springs are, as a matter of course, much smaller and weaker than those fitted to M.O. valves, and, in their case, it is all important that only a correct

THE ENGINE: FOUR-STROKE SYSTEM.

strength of spring should be employed. Experience shows that the best plan is to use as *strong* a spring as possible in the circumstances, a normal engine of 85 mm. bore requiring a spring exercising a resistance of from 3 to 4 lbs. against the suction for full opening. It must never be forgotten that the valve will have to be opened by the force of suction against the action of the spring, so one cannot be too careful in considering the adjustments necessary in the case of an automatic valve.

FIG. 11.—The Complete 3½ h.-p. " Peugeot " Power Unit.

Weak automatic inlet valve springs and a big opening mean sluggish running but more even firing at low speeds; while stronger springs and a restricted opening give greater speed and greater economy in petrol consumption; but it is not then an easy matter to keep the engine firing regularly while running slowly.

CHAPTER II.

THE ENGINE (*continued*): THE TWO-STROKE OR "VALVE-
LESS" SYSTEM.

MOTOR cycle engines constructed to work on the two-stroke (or double-impulse) system have now been on the market for some little time, but their manufacture is at present restricted to only one or two firms, who have, however, made them a success, and it is more than likely that in the near future the use of such engines will rapidly develop. Objections to the type formerly included faulty carburation, excessive petrol consumption, and a tendency to overheat. The first-named has been almost, if not entirely, overcome, and the second practically so; although it still remains the fact that two-stroke engines, as a rule, consume more petrol than a four-stroke one, the principal reason being, of course, that an explosion stroke occurs at every revolution of the flywheels instead of at every alternate one. The overheating trouble has been surmounted in one well-known design by introducing water-cooling, this design being illustrated in the present and succeeding chapters. Two-stroke engines as at present constructed do not require any distribution valves or timing gear, hence they are termed "valveless" engines, and much capital is made out of this point in their construction, which, as must be admitted, is a very good one. A valve or other device is provided for releasing the compression when starting up the engine; but this, of course, is totally apart from anything in the nature of a gear actuated inlet or exhaust valve.

The system of working in a two-stroke engine adapted to motor cycle practice is clearly shown in the accompanying diagrams, Fig. 12, for the use of which the author is indebted to the Scott Engineering Company, Ltd., of Bradford, who may be regarded as pioneers where the construction of such engines in a modern form is concerned. The Scott engine is of the three-ported valveless, two-stroke type, with twin

THE ENGINE: TWO-STROKE SYSTEM.

cylinders and water-cooling, thus combining features which represent ideals hitherto not considered altogether feasible for motor cycle purposes.

Diagram 1 shows the piston at the commencement of the power stroke as it begins to move downwards under the force of the explosion, whilst at the same time a carburetted mixture enters the crank-case at the inlet.

FIG. 12.—Diagrams showing Working Principle of "Scott" Two-stroke Engine.

Diagram 2 shows the piston at a lower point in the same stroke with expansion of the products of combustion in the cylinder, and the lower edge of the piston now covers up the inlet ports and thus cuts off all communication from the crank-case to the carburettor, so that the mixture begins to be compressed therein by the downward movement of the piston.

In Diagram 3 the top of the piston is seen uncovering the exhaust port, allowing the exhaust gases to escape to the

(A) (A)—Cylinders.
(B) (B)—Pistons.
(C) (C)—Conn. Rods.
(D) (D)—Water-cooled Heads.
(E) (E)—Bolts holding Heads to Cylinders.
(F)—Special Gudgeon Pin Fastening.
(L)—Flywheel.
(M) (M)—Roller Bearings.
(N)—High-speed Chain Wheel on Engine Shaft.
(O)—Low-speed Chain Wheel on Engine Shaft.
(Q) (Q)—Crank-cases.
(R) (R)—Balanced Crankshaft.
(S) (S) — Outer Aluminium Case connecting Engine to Frame.
(T) (T) — Gas Inlet Holes in Cylinder.
(V)—Water Connections.

Fig. 13.—Sectional Elevation of the "Scott" Two-stroke Twin-cylinder Water-cooled Engine.

silencer with an instant reduction of the pressure in the cylinder. At the same time, this further downward movement of the piston causes compression of the charge in the crank-case.

THE ENGINE: TWO-STROKE SYSTEM.   23

Diagram 4 shows the transfer port uncovered by the piston and the compressed charge in the crank-case blows through (by way of the transfer passage) and is deflected upwards by the peculiarly shaped deflector on the piston so that the remaining exhaust gases are swept out and the

(A)—Cylinder.
(B)—Piston.
(C)—Connecting Rod.
(D)—Water-Cooled Head.
(E)—Bolt holding Head to Cylinder.
(F)—Gudgeon Pin Fastening.
(H) (H)—Transfer Port.
(H¹)—Gas Inlet Port from Carburettor.
(J)—Exhaust Port.
(K)—Half - Compression Device.
(M)—Roller Bearings.
(Q) (Q)—Crank-cases.
(V) (V)—Water Connections.

FIG. 14.—Cross Section through "Scott" Two-stroke Engine.

cylinder is filled with a fresh charge of carburetted mixture. This is called the distribution period of the stroke, and the efficiency of the engine depends upon the design and provision for effective distribution.

FIG. 15.—External View of the "Scott" Two-stroke Twin-cylinder Water-cooled Engine, 3½-4 h.-p.

THE ENGINE: TWO-STROKE SYSTEM.

In Diagram 5, the piston is shown beginning to move upwards, first closing off the transfer port, whilst this upward movement creates a suction or partial vacuum in the crank-case.

Diagram 6: The piston moves further upwards and compresses the charge in the cylinder, with a corresponding increase in the crank-case suction until the lower edge of the piston again commences to uncover the inlet ports.

At this stage in the operation, if Diagram 1 is again consulted, it may be taken as showing the piston at the end of its upward compression stroke, while by the complete uncovering of the inlet ports the crank-case suction is fully open to the carburettor and by the flow of carburetted

FIG. 10.—Alternative Forms of "Scott" Pistons with Deflector Ledge.

mixture therefrom the vacuum in the crank-case is destroyed, and thus a fresh charge of mixture is drawn in ready to be compressed on the downward stroke of the piston and delivered to the cylinder as described by means of Diagram 4.

It will thus be gathered that whereas in the four-cycle engine the mixture is compressed in the cylinder head by the upward movement of the piston alone, in the two-stroke engine (shown by the diagrams) it is compressed in the crank-case by the downward movement of the same, and is then allowed to pass therefrom to the cylinder, above the piston, through the transfer passage, where it is again compressed into the cylinder head before being ignited. The piston itself alternately covers and uncovers the inlet, transfer and exhaust ports, and in so doing assumes the functions of the inlet and exhaust valves as well as its own. It is formed, as will be seen, with a deflecting ledge at the top; the purpose of which is to deflect the incoming gas towards the top of the cylinder. It also prevents, as far as possible, the mingling of the fresh with the waste gases. The Scott Engineering Company are the originators of this system, and as designed by them the sparking plug is caused to project into the purest part of the mixture.

Fig. 17.—The "Rex" Single-cylinder Two-stroke Engine.

The "Rex" two-stroke engine differs in point of detail from that described above. The drawings, showing the engine in part sectional elevation and end view, make the precise construction quite clear. The up stroke of the piston (O) induces a charge of gas from the carburettor, which communicates with a port in the cylinder walls through the inlet pipe (N). When the piston descends this charge is compressed in the crank-case, and at the moment the piston

THE ENGINE: TWO-STROKE SYSTEM.   27

arrives in the position in which it is shown—*i.e.*, with the gas inlet ports from the crank-case (I.I.) in register with the transfer port into the cylinder above the piston—the next upward stroke of the piston compresses the charge ready for firing and at the same time induces a fresh charge of gas into the crank-case, the exhaust gas escaping at the same time as the entry into the cylinder of the fresh charge takes place. The exhaust port (E) is in the right side of the cylinder and the piston head is shaped as in the previous case so that it deflects the incoming gas towards the top of the cylinder.

The pipe (H) which connects the transfer port with the top of the cylinder has at the top a compression release valve (F) operated by a Bowden wire and cable (G) which is connected to a lever on the handle-bar. When this valve is opened the gas compressed in the top of the cylinder is released and returned to the crank-case by way of the transfer ports. Examination of the drawings will show that when the piston is at the top of the stroke—*i.e.*, in the act of compressing the charge in the cylinder—and the release valve is open, the base of the piston has uncovered the ports of the transfer passage and there is a free path from the top of the cylinder into the crank-case by way of the return pipe (H). The "Rex" two-stroke engines are air-cooled only, and are made both with a single and with twin cylinders.

The Two-stroke and Four-stroke Systems Compared.

Before leaving the subject of two-stroke engines and the point as to the increased petrol consumption associated with them in the minds of those who study these things, it may be well to draw a few comparisons in this respect between such engines and those which work upon the four-stroke principle. If we take for this purpose a twin-cylinder engine of each type having a cylinder capacity of 27 cub. ins. we find, in the first place, that owing to the fact that in the two-stroke type a certain proportion of stroke is lost owing to the piston functioning as a valve, the actual effective stroke instead of being $2\frac{1}{2}$ ins. is $1\frac{7}{8}$ ins.; hence the actual displacement of the cylinders is 20 cub. ins. instead of 27 cub. ins.; but, seeing that the charge is drawn into the crank-case, we have to compare the displacement of the crank-case with that of the cylinders in the four-stroke type.

28 THE MOTOR CYCLIST'S HANDBOOK.

FIG. 18.—Indicator Diagram from "Scott" Engine.

FIG. 19.—Indicator Diagram from "Scott" Engine.

The effective stroke in the crank-case is, in the two-stroke engine, also $1\frac{7}{8}$ ins., so that the total cubic displacement is only 20 cub. ins. instead of 27 cub. ins., and if the two engines are to be compared on the same basis, it is necessary to compare a two-stroke engine having a 20 cub. ins. crank-case displacement with a four-stroke engine having the same cylinder displacement. This, in the author's view, is a very important fact, for it will be seen that the result of the reduced displacement is, of course, to make the mean effective pressure of the two-stroke engine considerably below that of the four-stroke, and whereas in the latter the M.E.P. ranges from 60 to 80 lbs. per sq. in. that in the best designed two-stroke (of course, without additional scavenger pumps) is from 40 to 50 lbs., according to the speed.

This loss is, of course, largely due to the reduced displacement arising from the less effective stroke. Another very important point is that at very high speeds the M.E.P. falls much more quickly in the case of the two-stroke than in the four-stroke type of engine, although, on the other hand, at slow speeds, the M.E.P. is increased and very nearly approaches that in the four-stroke type. The accompanying diagrams, Figs. 18 and 19, are constructed from actual diagrams taken from a "Scott" two-stroke engine.

The whole bearing of these remarks upon petrol consumption is that it cannot reasonably be expected that the two-stroke engine should give anything like double the power of a four-stroke, although its power strokes are doubled, and the best that can be expected is that it should give double the power of an engine comparing with it on the same effective displacement.

CHAPTER III.

Twin- and Four-cylinder Motor Cycle Engines (Four-stroke System).

The object in augmenting the number of cylinders in a petrol motor is, to some great extent, although by no means entirely, that of obtaining increased power; but, in any case, whether the engine is of increased horse-power or not, when

Fig. 20.—First Stage of Cycle, Twin-cylinder Four-stroke Engine.

the driving force is distributed over two or more pistons instead of being concentrated on one alone, superior balance, lighter individual parts, and a much more efficient turning

THE ENGINE: TWIN- AND FOUR-CYLINDER ENGINES. 31

moment is secured, while starting is facilitated and there is greater flexibility and more rapid acceleration from a low speed.

In twin-cylinder engines the cylinders are usually placed so as to form a "V" longitudinally with the run of the machine, and so that they follow the contour of the frame, with the carburettor placed between the cylinders, and this

FIG. 21.—Second Stage of Cycle, Twin-cylinder Four-stroke Engine.

forms a convenient and well-disposed arrangement, and as the crank-case remains of the same width as in a single-cylinder motor, the whole fits in place very snugly and is well adapted to the circumstances of the design. The cylinders are placed at varying angles to one another, but generally somewhere between 45 degs. and 90 degs., and the arrangement is usually such that when one piston is commencing its suction stroke the other is nearing the end of its compression stroke, so that ignition takes place in the latter when the former has performed some part of its suction stroke. Then, as the No. 1 piston commences to rise for compressing the charge it has drawn into the cylinder, the No. 2 piston is just about completing its working stroke, and, a moment later, will be travelling upwards again on the

Fig. 22.—Third Stage of Cycle, Twin-cylinder Four-stroke Engine.

exhaust stroke; the exhaust valve having meanwhile commenced to open just before the piston began to ascend.

In the diagram (Fig. 20) on page 30, which shows an engine with its cylinders at 90 degs. apart, the piston in No. 1 cylinder is about to descend on the suction stroke, while that in No. 2 cylinder has very nearly reached the

THE ENGINE: TWIN- AND FOUR-CYLINDER ENGINES. 33

end of its compression stroke. Then in Fig. 21 No. 1 piston is rising to compress the charge, and No. 2 is practically at the end of its firing stroke, and its exhaust valve is just about to open. In this way half of the complete cycle has been performed.

In Fig. 22 ignition has just taken place in No. 1 cylinder,

FIG. 23.—Final Stage of Cycle, Twin-cylinder Four-stroke Engine.

and in No. 2 the piston has reached a point near the end of its exhaust stroke; while in the final diagram (Fig. 23) No. 1 piston is exhausting an exploded charge, and No. 2 piston is drawing in a fresh one, and the four-cycle system being now completed, the same round of operations re-commences.

D

Twin-cylinder engines of the "V" type are very often indeed fitted with automatic inlet valves, and the valve operating mechanism is thus reduced to a single cam gear for each exhaust valve, and in some engines one cam is alone made to do duty for both exhaust valves, so that the gear mechanism for the mechanically-operated valves is actually more simple than in most single-cylinder engines. In such designs the cam, together with the timing gear wheel, is mounted on or formed in one piece with a short projecting

FIG. 24.—"Rex" Twin-cylinder V Type Engine (Overhead M.O.I.V.).

shaft or spindle midway between the two tappets, and actuates each rocker arm in turn. Where mechanically-operated valves are fitted throughout, however, two cam gears at least must be employed, while in a few cases, not perhaps of recent pattern, each of the four valves has its own independent cam. In Figs. 28A and 28B is shown an arrangement of overhead mechanical valves as applied to a "J.A.P." V type twin engine.

In a few designs of twin-cylinder motor cycle engines

THE ENGINE: TWIN- AND FOUR-CYLINDER ENGINES. 35

the cylinders are placed side by side transversely to the frame. This plan has been successfully applied to small engines for driving lightweight machines. The explosions take place alternately in each cylinder and the pistons rise and fall in unison the one with the other. The "Scott" two-stroke engine has its cylinders placed side by side in an inclined position, but in this case the pistons are always travelling in opposite directions.

In another plan—as yet adopted by one well-known firm only—the cylinders are carried in an end-to-end position so that the pistons are horizontally opposed to one another.

FIG. 25.—The "Douglas" Twin-cylinder Engine with Horizontally Opposed Cylinders.

This is the "Douglas" twin motor of $2\frac{3}{4}$ h.-p. The flywheel is on the outside of the crank-case, as shown in the sectional drawing (Fig. 28), in which the precise design of the crankshaft can also be seen. This arrangement of cylinders necessitates a special means of operating the exhaust valves, the features of which may be likewise gathered from the drawings. The cam acts upon the end of a horizontal tappet rod, which in turn actuates a horizontal spindle (in reality an adjustable tappet rod) and motion is conveyed by the reciprocating movement of the latter to a bell-crank placed

36 THE MOTOR CYCLIST'S HANDBOOK.

FIG. 26.
The Moving Parts of the "Douglas" Engine.

(A)(A)—Cylinders.
(B)—Piston.
(C)—Conn. Rod.
(D)—Crank-shaft.
(E)—Inlet Port.
(F)—Inlet Valve.
(G)—Exhaust Valve.

(H) — Exhaust Port.
(I) (K)—Valve Lifting Mechanism.
(L)—Flywheel.

FIG. 27.—The "Douglas" Engine in Horizontal Section.

THE ENGINE: TWIN- AND FOUR-CYLINDER ENGINES.

at its outer extremity, which effects the necessary lifting of the valve itself, which is placed vertically, as shown, with the automatic inlet valve above it. These engines have proved very successful, and have many excellent points in their design.

A few manufacturers adopt a slightly different arrangement of "V" engine, in which the front cylinder follows the alignment of the down tube of the frame, while the rear cylinder is quite vertical, the object sought being a more thorough cooling of the latter cylinder which is not then shielded from the air currents (as in other types) by the one in front of it.

FIG. 28.—Vertical Cross Section of the "Douglas" Engine.
(A)—Cylinder opening; (D)—Crankshaft; (L)—Flywheel; (M)—Belt Pulley; (S)—Magneto.

Yet another type of twin engines is the new Premier, a 45-deg. engine with cylinders firing at regular intervals. It should be explained that the ordinary "V" type of engine with cylinders set at 45 degs. has what is known as a long and a short firing interval—that is, one explosion turns the flywheels more than a complete revolution, while the other turns them less than a complete revolution, both connecting-rods operating on the same crank-pin. In the Premier engine, however, the connecting-rods do not operate on the same crank-pin, but each works on an independent bearing, the front rod being something in the shape of a fork or eccentric strap and mounted on bearings on large bosses formed on the insides of the flywheels, and the rear connecting-rod direct on to the crank pin, as in ordinary practice.

Fig. 28A.
Overhead M.O. Valves fitted to "J.A.P." Twin Engine.

Fig. 28B.
"J.A.P." V Type Twin Engine with Overhead M.O. Inlet and Exhaust Valves.

THE ENGINE: TWIN- AND FOUR-CYLINDER ENGINES. 39

The drawing reproduced herewith shows the action within the two cylinders in completing a complete revolution, each one before its companion cylinder fires. The two cranks reach their respective dead centres simultaneously, and the centre lines of the cylinders and that of the crank-case are all in the same plane, the resultant force of each explosion transmitted to the crankshaft being exerted centrally. With this arrangement even firing intervals and central balancing are obtained, and it is immaterial at what angle to each other the axes of the cylinders are placed. The bore and stroke of this engine are 66 mm. by 80 mm., giving a cubic capacity of 548 c.c. and a nominal horse-power of $3\frac{3}{4}$ h.-p.

FIG. 29.—The New "Premier" Engine with Cylinders at 45°, and Special Crank-Pin Arrangement, with even Firing Intervals.

Except in the case of a few powerful racing machines—mostly of foreign origin and designed for track racing purposes—three-cylinder motor cycle engines are unknown, but four-cylinder ones have proved highly successful, although, as goes without saying, they are necessarily more complicated than other types.

FIG. 30. Enlarged Sectional View of the Connecting Rod Arrangement in "Premier" 3¾ h.-p. V Type Engine.

THE ENGINE: TWIN- AND FOUR-CYLINDER ENGINES. 41

Fig. 30A.—External View of the "Premier" Engine.

Fig. 31.—A "Wanderer" Twin Motor with Vertical Rear Cylinder.

Four-cylinder Motor Cycle Engines.

The principal claims put forward on behalf of the four-cylinder engine are: absence of engine vibration, remarkable ease of starting, and great flexibility, combined with a positive driving effort, the latter in consequence of the fact that a shaft and bevel drive is employed instead of a belt or chain. A four-cylinder motor cycle with variable-speed gear fitted is probably the most luxurious among single-track machines. It requires intelligent handling, and a

FIG. 32. The Latest "F.N." Four-cylinder Motor Cycle Engine in Sectional Elevation.

(See also FIG. 33 for lettering.)

(O)—Flywheel.
(P)—Crankshaft.
(Q)—Electric Current Distributor.

careful eye to its maintenance; but in return it provides a most delightful form of locomotion, and is very steady and comfortable to ride upon. Illustrated particulars of the "F.N." and "T.A.C." four-cylinder engines (the most advanced examples of standard construction as yet produced) are appended, and from these a good idea of the appearance and characteristics of four-cylinder motor bicycles may be obtained.

THE ENGINE: TWIN-AND FOUR-CYLINDER ENGINES. 43

(A)—Cylinders.
(B)—Pistons.
(C)—Conn. Rod.
(D)—Crank Chamber (Upper).
(E)—Crank Chamber (Lower).
(F)—Inlet Pipe.
(G)—Exhaust Pipe.
(H)—A.O. Inlet Valve
(I)—Exhaust Valve.
(J)—Valve Tappet.
(K)—Rocking Lever Lifting Tappet.
(L)—Cam and Shaft.
(M)—Gudgeon Pin.
(N)—Sparking Plug.

FIG. 33.—End View of the "F.N." Four-cylinder Engine; "A.O.I.V." open; Piston on Suction Stroke.

Fig. 34.—The "T.A.C." Four-cylinder Engine.

Fig. 35.—End View of the "T.A.C." Four-cylinder Engine.

CHAPTER IV.

Constructional Details of Motor Cycle Engines.

Cylinder and Piston.

The cylinder of a motor cycle engine is constructed of close-grained cast-iron, and, in 90 per cent. of cases, in one piece, although a very few makers still adhere to the practice of forming the combustion head separately, with the idea of providing greater access to the piston and cylinder. The

Fig. 36.—Sectional View of Piston, "Rex" Motor Cycle Engine, designed for two Piston Rings near top.

Fig. 37.—"Wanderer" Piston with Ring encircling ends of Gudgeon Pin.

cylinder is provided on the outside with a number of radiating fins or ribs, so that a largely increased surface may be available for cooling purposes as the motor passes through the air, and by this means the heat generated as the result of the continuous explosions taking place within the cylinder is dissipated to a considerable degree; hence the use of the term "air-cooled" motors.

The piston is made of cast-iron (although in a few cases of steel), and is fitted, as a rule, with three rings located in grooves near the top; but more recently it has become the fashion with some makers to employ only two rings, placed sometimes close together near the top of the piston, and at other times with one ring at the top and the other one near the base of the piston. For this last-named plan it is claimed that the movement of the piston is steadied, and that leakage of the compression is more completely obviated. It is also claimed that the use of two piston rings greatly reduces the cylinder friction and, consequently, increases the engine power, and as there is naturally

FIG. 38.
Piston with Stepped Rings.   Piston with Stepped Rings and Retaining Pins.

a smaller surface area in contact with the cylinder walls (where only two rings are employed) it seems a not unreasonable assertion. There appears to be little wrong with the three-ring method, however, when the parts are properly designed and fitted. A motor cycle recently acquired by the author has the piston fitted with two rings near the top and one near the bottom, the latter acting only as a guide, and the piston is perforated above it to assist lubrication. Some makers form the rings with square cut or "stepped" slots, and sometimes a tiny pin is inserted in the groove to keep the ring from revolving around the piston. This is undoubtedly good practice, for, should the rings

CONSTRUCTIONAL DETAILS OF MOTOR CYCLE ENGINES. 47

work into such a position that the slots are in line, some loss of compression will almost certainly follow. In the case of the stepped-slot and pin method this, of course, becomes impossible.

Properly fitting piston rings, possessing a suitable degree of elasticity, are perfectly compression tight, and will give long service without any bother in a correctly lubricated cylinder. The top of the piston is, as a rule, flat; but in some cases slightly domed. This latter form adds to the strength of the construction, and may also prevent, to some extent, the accumulation of burnt oil or "carbonised deposits" on the piston head, owing to the fact that the

Fig. 39.—Gudgeon Pin Fastening : " J.A.P." Engines.

lubricating oil which has worked past the piston rings tends to drain off the domed-shaped top on to the cylinder walls instead of collecting in the centre of the piston as when the latter is flat topped.

The Connecting-Rod and Gudgeon Pin.

The connecting-rod is usually a steel stamping with bushed ends. It is secured within the piston at its upper extremity by means of a gudgeon pin running crosswise from one side to the other. The piston is provided with a short internal sleeve on each side, and the ends of the gudgeon pin are held securely in these sleeves by being driven tightly into place with a $\frac{1}{1000}$ degree of taper, while in several different types of makers' engines setscrews are used as an additional means of securing parallel gudgeon pins. It is good practice maybe to take the additional precaution in the latter circumstances of fitting these setscrews; but the author once had a piston entirely ruined by a screw working loose and, in falling, getting fixed between the piston and the top of the crank-case, the result being a smashed piston. In another engine he drove for some 30,000

Fig. 40.—Latest method of securing Gudgeon Pin; "Peugeot" Motor Cycle Engine.

miles, and which had twin-cylinders, the gudgeon pins were held by taper drive only, there was never any trouble from start to finish, and the pins never worked the slightest bit loose.

One well-known firm of motor cycle engine makers adopts a setscrew of large diameter, and further secures this by a pin passing right through the screw and the sleeve of the piston, a plan which, they say, has never been known

CONSTRUCTIONAL DETAILS OF MOTOR CYCLE ENGINES. 49

to fail. A sketch of this arrangement is appended, Fig. 39. The upper end of the connecting-rod engages with the open portion of the gudgeon pin, between the internal sleeves of the piston; the pin itself being, of course, held stationary, while the rod swings or vibrates upon it. A gun-metal or phosphor-bronze bush takes the wear between the two surfaces. The arrangement shown in Fig. 37 is employed in another well-known make of engine. The gudgeon is

FIG. 41.—The Connecting Rods of a Twin-cylinder " V " Type Motor Cycle Engine.

a driving fit in the piston, and a ring is fitted which covers both ends of the pin to prevent any possible scoring of the cylinder walls. The latest " Peugeot " motor cycle engine has external recesses on each side of the piston, and the gudgeon is secured by a tapered pin and castle nut with spring washer as seen in Fig. 40.

In the majority of twin engines one of the connecting-rods is forked at the lower end, while the other rod has a single end which fits in between the arms of the fork, and both rods work on a common crank-pin as in Fig. 41. An exception is the new " Premier " engine illustrated and described on page 40.

E

Flywheels and their Components.

The flywheels are made as large as contingencies allow, and with heavy rims, so that full advantage may be taken of the force of momentum imparted to them during the working stroke, which motion is relied upon to keep the piston, valves, etc., acting during the remaining strokes. With heavy flywheels the engine will continue working for a much longer period after power is shut off by virtue of this stored up momentum, and will also run with regularity at a much lower speed than would be possible with lighter and smaller flywheels; this steadiness and uniformity of

FIG. 42.—Flywheels and Connecting Rod of " Arno " 3 h.-p. Engine. Each Flywheel with Engine Shaft a Solid Steel Stamping.

running, and the reduced vibration which accompanies it, is in fact a principal aim of the designer when calculating the proportion and weight of the various parts. The size and weight of the flywheels depend, of course, on the size of the cylinder and piston, the whole having to be carefully

CONSTRUCTIONAL DETAILS OF MOTOR CYCLE ENGINES. 51

computed so that an even balancing of the reciprocating and revolving parts may be assured. The flywheels of the "Arno" engines are steel stampings with thin centres and heavy rims, the main shaft being stamped out in one piece with the flywheel (see Fig. 42).

The crank-pin bridges the space between the flywheels and takes the lower end of the connecting-rod in a phosphor-bronze bearing, similar to that of the gudgeon pin, but of larger dimensions. The main bearings of the engine shaft are carried in the sides of the crank-case, which are considerably thickened at these points or made with a projection on the outside so as to provide as long a bearing as possible. In some engines ball-bearings are fitted to the main shaft to further assist in overcoming frictional resistance, and thereby securing greater continuity and uniformity of rotation. Ball-bearing engines are very "lively" ones as a rule—that is, they run with remarkable freedom and dash, and the increased flexibility is especially advantageous when a lot of variation in the speed is required for traffic or other reasons.

The Crank-case and Timing Gear Chamber.

The crank-case itself is formed in two halves, and is, in the majority of cases, made of aluminium alloy, for the sake of lightness, but iron or steel crank-cases are by no means unknown. It is (or should be) perfectly oil-tight—that is, the joint with the cylinder, as well as that between the two halves of the case itself, should be capable of retaining oil. The joint between the base of the cylinder and the top of the crank-case can be quite efficiently made with brown paper soaked in thick oil, fish glue, or other similar composition. Some motor cyclists use Seccotine and other preparations of the same character, and then when they desire to remove the cylinder for inspection or cleaning purposes, it sometimes sticks with an obstinate tenacity, such as is highly conducive to bad temper. A thin jointing of aluminium sheet makes a good packing, but it costs more than brown paper or any of the rubberised steam packings, and sometimes cracks, and is not then of much use for the purpose. The joints between the sparking plug and the cylinder, and also those of the valve caps and compression tap are best when consisting of copper and asbestos washers, which are both highly efficient and cheap to buy. The crank-case is fitted on its underside with a drain tap for use when running off used-up lubricating oil and when flushing out with paraffin. A non-return ball valve is sometimes screwed into the crank-case to allow of the air compressed therein escaping; in some engines this compressed air escapes through the hollow main shaft.

The timing gears are carried in a separate chamber to themselves, known as the distribution chamber, on the outside of the crank-case, where they are easily accessible, and from which position the driving of the magneto is most readily arranged for. The timing gear wheels are of case-hardened steel with teeth cut from the solid blank, the rocking lever or roller between cam and tappet being also of steel. The cam or " half-time " gear spindle of either the inlet or exhaust valve is generally made taper at the outer end, and on to this tapered portion is secured, by means of a feather, the gear-wheel or sprocket for imparting primary motion to the magneto drive. Outside the taper again is a threaded portion so that the gear-wheel may be locked in position by means of a nut. The magneto, to which detailed reference is made in the chapter on "Ignition," has a corresponding gear-wheel or sprocket on the end of its armature shaft, and these two wheels—one on the engine half-time shaft and the other on the magneto armature shaft—are connected up either by intermediate gear-wheels or a chain.

Inlet and Exhaust Valves.

The inlet and exhaust valves when mechanically operated are of the general formation shown in Fig. 43. The stem is thickened for some distance below the head of the valve for strengthening purposes. This enlarged portion of the stem works in a guide cast with the cylinder or screwed in place below the valve chamber for steadying the valve and ensuring a true vertical movement of the same. At its lower end the valve stem has a slot cut in it for taking a key or wedge, the function of which is to hold the cap in which the spring rests at its base and prevent the spring from falling. The spring, as already shown, exercises a good deal of control over the movement of the valve after it has been lifted from its seating by the cam, and, when of accurate strength, ensures a prompt and even return of the valve to its seating.

CONSTRUCTIONAL DETAILS OF MOTOR CYCLE ENGINES. 53

The cam, as before pointed out, has to operate against the power of this spring ; but without the latter there would be no certainty or regularity in the valve movements.

The cam acts on a tappet rod which in turn raises the valve, and it is very important that the tappet should be a true and easy (but not slack) fit in its guide, so that it may move quite freely but yet not allow oil to escape from the crank-case through the guide. The tappet rod usually has a disc or " table " head, which tends to distribute the wear between it and the foot of the valve stem instead of such wear being concentrated on one fixed point all the time ; it also ensures that an even contact between the two parts will be permanently maintained.

It is even more important still that the valve stems be an accurate fit, in *their* guides, as, owing to the considerable heat which is imparted to them, expansion takes place, and unless this were duly allowed for (it sometimes is *not*), the valves will stick in their guides and then there is an end for the time being to the proper working of the engine.

As before said, the valve springs must be correctly proportioned to suit the particular engine to which they are applied, and when it becomes necessary, as in course of time it must do, to replace them, the best plan by far is to obtain the new springs direct from the makers of the engine rather than to select them haphazard on the " nearly as possible the same " principle. The difference in the performance of an engine when the springs are of proper strength and in good condition, and when the opposite is the case, is a very appreciable one indeed ; and often, when the rider has exhausted all his endeavours in trying to find out the cause of unsatisfactory running, a simple replacement of the valve springs will work wonders, immediately restoring the lost power and " life " of the engine. Mechanically-operated valves

FIG. 43.
Mechanically operated Valve of Motor Cycle Engine.

are, as a rule, made in one piece, of nickel steel, with the heads as large as circumstances permit, so that the free passage of the gases may be assured, without its being necessary to provide a big lift. The stem is also of substantial proportions in good class engines, and the whole is turned out in accurately finished style, which is more than could have been said a few years ago where certain makes were concerned. Some makers fit their valves with cast-iron heads, and others with cast-iron rings to form seatings.

Automatic inlet valves work with the head downwards and the short stem pointing vertically above them, as illustrated in Fig. 33, page 43. In this type the seating is removable

FIG. 44.—A Motor Cycle Engine Dissected ; The "Norton" 3½-4 h.-p.

with the valve itself, this greatly facilitating the adjustment or grinding of the valve, the latter operation being very rarely needed, but the former one frequently so. The guide for the stem is in one with the seating, and the latter screws into the combustion chamber in the top of the cylinder above the exhaust valve pocket. The spring and stem are retained in their correct relative positions by various means, either a cup and cotter being used much as in mechanically-operated valves, or else the valve stem is screw-threaded and

CONSTRUCTIONAL DETAILS OF MOTOR CYCLE ENGINES. 55

the parts are secured by means of locknuts. The method of fixing and adjusting the valves is described later in Chapter XI, which deals with Overhauling and Tuning up the Engine.

The inlet valve chamber is in communication with the induction pipe, to the other end of which the carburettor is attached, while the exhaust valve chamber has a branch to which the exhaust pipe is attached, and by means of which the burnt products of combustion pass away to the silencer and finally into the atmosphere.

Cylinder Mountings.

An opening is formed in the combustion head of the cylinder, and this is screwed to receive a, compression tap to allow of the "compression" being released if desired, and also for injecting petrol or paraffin into the cylinder to facilitate starting the engine in cold weather, should the piston have become somewhat "gummed" up by the film of congealed lubricating oil which sets between itself and the cylinder walls. This tap is seldom used for the purpose of releasing the compression, that operation being much more conveniently achieved by means of the exhaust valve lifter, a device which permits of the exhaust valve being lifted from its seating altogether independently of the cam, so that the compression escapes down the exhaust pipe until the valve is dropped on to its seating by the release of the lifter handle. A second screwed opening in the cylinder head takes the threaded shank of the sparking plug, communication between which and the accumulator or magneto is established by means of a high-tension cable for the conveyance of current for igniting the charge by means of an electric spark, the whole of these details being either separately or collectively illustrated in one portion or another of these pages.

Exhaust Pipe, Silencer, and Cut-out.

The exhaust pipe communicates, at its upper extremity, with the exhaust valve chamber and delivers the burnt gases to the silencer below, the passage of which into the atmosphere is retarded somewhat by means of baffle-plates, cups, or other means of breaking up the discharged volume into particles before allowing of final escape. Very much indeed depends upon the design of the exhaust pipe (which should be of ample area and free from sharp bends), and more still upon the design of the silencer itself; for if the opposition to the free egress of the exhaust gases is too strict, the latter, so to speak, become trapped and are unable to get clear with sufficient rapidity, with the result that back pressure is set up; the engine overheats, and loses power. A reasonable degree of silence is highly to be desired, but if it be accompanied with anything more than a slight

FIG. 45.—Path of Exhaust gases through Clair Silencer.

amount of back pressure, then it is dearly bought. The accompanying drawing shows one of the well-known "Clair" silencers, the efficiency of which has now been fully established. It will be seen that the silencer chamber contains a number of cups, each having a number of small holes, and the path of the gases is clearly shown from the cylinder to

CONSTRUCTIONAL DETAILS OF MOTOR CYCLE ENGINES. 57

Fig. 45A.—Exhaust Cut-out arrangement for two separate Silencers.

Fig. 45B.—A Simple form of Cut-out where both Exhaust Pipes Lead to the same Silencer.

the atmosphere. In the author's experience the use of the "Clair" silencer gives a remarkable degree of silence, devoid of back pressure altogether. The gases are afforded a free exit without being allowed to escape until well broken up, and then at a low velocity.

Some "silencers" are unworthy of the name; but others, while being of very simple construction (consisting merely of a plain exhaust box with a perforated tube inside, through which the gases first pass before entering the silencer proper, and from the latter out through a second series of openings), give quite good results. The addition of a length of piping with flattened end to the silencer sometimes aids matters, and the escape holes are not then required. Many manufacturers of motor cycles equip the silencer with a "cut-out," which may be opened and closed by the rider at will. When opened the escape of the gases is largely facilitated, and there is a corresponding increase in the noise occasioned, but the engine usually accelerates, and will, as a rule, climb a hill better when the cut-out is open than when it is closed. The indiscriminate use of the exhaust cut-out when passing through towns, or, indeed, at any time other than when riding on an open country road, is to be largely deprecated. In the case of twin-cylinder motor cycle engines a separate silencer may be used for each cylinder or the two exhaust pipes may be led into one common silencer. Cut-out devices adaptable to both types of construction are shown in the accompanying sketches (**Figs. 45A** and **45B**).

The latter method is more commonly resorted to nowadays, possibly because it simplifies the construction. Provided that the correct volume of space is assured, it, perhaps, matters little whether one or two silencers are used. The single silencer plan facilitates the fitting of an exhaust cut-out on a twin engine.

CONSTRUCTIONAL DETAILS OF MOTOR CYCLE ENGINES. 59

FIG. 45C.—The "Premier" $3\frac{1}{2}$ h.-p. Single-cylinder Engine with Auxiliary Exhaust Port and two Exhaust Pipes.

CHAPTER V.

COMPRESSION.

HAVING now considered the working principle of the engine—both in its four-stroke and two-stroke forms—and also the general features of design and construction, it will be useful to turn our attention to the all-important subject of Compression, upon which phase of its being the petrol engine depends so largely for its efficiency. We have already seen that, after the gaseous mixture from the carburettor has been drawn into the cylinder on the suction stroke, the following upward stroke of the piston compresses it into the restricted space known as the combustion chamber at the top of the cylinder, so that, as before explained, the explosion may be greatly magnified in force, and it will be readily understood that, unless every part of the cylinder and its components be made gas-tight, the compressed gases will leak through and be lost in part for the purpose of driving the engine.

Loss of compression occurs when the piston rings do not spring out all round to tightly fit the cylinder walls, or when the valves, especially the exhaust, does not bed down properly in its seating. A very hot crank-case is a sure indication that the piston rings are a bad fit, and allowing compressed gas or air to leak past them. The joints between cylinder and the compression tap, sparking plug, and valve caps must all be securely made to resist leakage, and, of course, there must be no crack of any sort in the cylinder casting extending to the interior.

In course of time, when the engine has done a considerable amount of work, the exhaust valve face becomes worn and " pitted " with small indentations, resulting from the contact of the valve with burnt gases at a very high temperature, and when this stage is reached, it becomes necessary to grind the valve carefully in its seating until a smooth and even surface between the two has been restored—a very easy, if somewhat laborious and tedious, process. Once done

—and carefully done—further loss of compression in this direction is, for a considerable period of working, wholly prevented, and if not then entirely satisfactory, other causes must be looked for in the directions indicated above.

When all the points at which compression can leak away are made sound and in good order, the piston rings springing out and forming a true contact all round with the cylinder walls, with the gap in the rings not more than $\frac{1}{64}$ in., valves an accurate fit in their seatings, and all the other parts well conditioned, then the engine is sure to have a good compression, and one which should withstand the weight of the rider suspended on the pedal while the rear wheel is jacked up off the ground for at least 30 seconds, or, when pushed along the road, skid the back wheel as the highest point of compression is reached. With the compression in good order, the engine will start more readily, and will perform in better style on hills. Even a slight loss of compression will affect its working, although, maybe, not very noticeably; but if the leakage be at all serious, it may become a difficult matter to get any really useful work from the engine, except under the most easy and favourable circumstances. Leakage of compression is more serious at low than at high speeds, as then the power developed by the engine is in any case less than when running fast.

The Ratio of Compression.

In addition to the question of good or bad compression, there also arises that of *high* and *low* compression—another matter altogether. A high-compression engine is one in which the cylinder combustion chamber or compression space is restricted in volume more than is usual, so that the gases are more tightly compressed than where the volume is larger. The ratio of compression depends very largely upon the purpose for which the engine is required, and the degree is also affected by valve areas and timings, combustion chamber design, and flywheel diameter and weight. For very smooth and quiet running a compression ratio as low as 35 lbs. has given very good results, although, with this compression, it becomes necessary to ignite the charge much earlier than is usual. For all-round purposes a ratio of 3 to 1—that is, cylinder capacity three times that of the combustion chamber —has proved very satisfactory.

With this compression fairly high speeds may be obtained, and, generally speaking, the engine will plug up a long hill, as well as potter along very slowly if required to do so. This ratio is a much favoured one with motor cycle manufacturers for touring machines, and the majority of them probably work within a few pounds of it. There is, no doubt, some advantage to be gained in the direction of economy and speed by using an exceptionally high compression if the aim is short-distance bursts of speed only, as in competition work, for example ; but for continued running the heat generated is such as to absolutely prohibit any continuation of running with a wide throttle, if the compression is anything over 90 lbs. Above this ratio the mean working pressure does not increase in proportion to the amount of compression, and a great deal of negative work is thrown on to the engine.

A compression of 90 lbs. in an air-cooled engine makes it impossible for a well-warmed engine to take full advantage of throttle opening, as the expansion caused by the heat generated by the work done in compressing the charge brings the pressure so high as to nearly approximate to that due to the explosion ; in fact, the charge is frequently ignited previous to the piston completing the compression stroke, and what is called " knocking " then takes place. The burning of the charge under these circumstances may almost be likened to detonation, as compared with the expansive push really required.

The effect of compression alone in increasing the rate of combustion is due to the fact that particles of the various gases of which the explosive mixture is composed are then in much closer intimacy. This is not the only advantage of compression in a petrol engine. Other advantages are that, with a given engine stroke, there is a large change of volume between maximum compression and the end of the stroke. Also that, by compressing the gas, a large weight of gas is contained in a small volume, so that the distance through which combustion has to extend is small, and the amount of cooling surface retarding combustion is also small. The degree to which it is advisable to carry compression is to some extent limited by fear of producing a jerky engine, but chiefly by the possibility of self-ignition of the gas before the proper moment, owing to the heat produced by compression.

CHAPTER VI.

THE CARBURETTOR.

THE carburettor (or vaporiser), although not exactly a part of the engine itself, occupies a position of the greatest importance in relation thereto ; indeed, it may be said that the efficiency of the engine (assuming the other parts to be in order) depends primarily upon this relatively small device, the function of which is to feed the mixture or fuel, for consumption in the engine, in the right proportions as regards its constituent elements and to maintain a continuous and sufficient supply.

In other words, the carburettor is a device in which the petrol delivered from the tank is turned into a highly gaseous vapour by its mixture with air, and, unless the mixing process is performed with accuracy and in the right proportions, faulty working of the engine follows as a matter of course. In general outward and detailed design different makes of carburettors vary considerably ; but the main operative principle remains the same in all cases, so that a brief description of the principle of carburation, in conjunction with some examples from present-day practice in the design and construction of the apparatus, will suffice to make clear what the carburettor is and how its functions are performed.

Spray and Surface Carburettors.

The modern carburettor, as applied to motor cycle engines, is invariably of what is known as the " spray " type—that is to say, the petrol is delivered to the chamber in which the mixture with air is to be effected in the form of spray or a stream of small particles ; whereas, in the old surface carburettor, formerly always used, the petrol collected within a chamber in a pool and the current of air was so arranged as to be drawn over its surface and so to set up the process of vaporisation.

Some of these carburettors had wicks for soaking up the petrol, thus increasing the surface exposed to the air, and there may also have been other methods designed to effect

Fig. 46.—The "B. & B." 1910 Carburettor in Sectional Elevation.

the same purpose. Whatever they were, however, they have now all given way to the spray form of construction which, although perhaps necessitating a rather more complicated apparatus for its accomplishment, takes up less room and is doubtless better suited to modern requirements.

Construction and Working of the Spray Type.

The spray carburettor consists in the main of two separate portions—*i.e.*, the float chamber, and the mixing or spraying chamber. Petrol from the tank passes down through the petrol pipe (A) to the float chamber (B).

In this chamber, as its name implies, there is a float which consists of a hollow brass body or drum, through the centre of which there passes in a vertical direction a long thin rod, known as the needle valve. The base of this needle is tapered to a point, and this conical portion fits into a tapered opening through which the petrol rises into the float chamber. The function of the needle valve and float is to control the feed of petrol from the pipe communicating with the main tank, and the manner in which this function is performed may be briefly described as follows:—

FIG. 47.—The "B. & B." 1910 Carburettor, with Handle-Bar Fittings.

Near its upper extremity the needle has affixed to it a grooved collar (D) with which there engages a pair of small brass balance weights (EE), each pivoting on a small split pin and held securely in position by a bracket through which the split pins also pass, and which is itself secured to the cover or lid of the float chamber. The needle rests at the top in a tubular sleeve raised above the cover and, as seen, clearance is left above the needle so that the latter has space in which to rise. When the petrol reaches the base of the float chamber it passes directly into the chamber itself, causing the float to rise and to continue doing so until the two brass weights (EE), which are pushed upwards by the ascending float, are raised to a predetermined height, at which point they automatically cut off further supply by forcing the needle down on to its seating and the further delivery of petrol is for the time being cut off. The passage (F) forms a means of communication between the float chamber and spraying chamber. Here the petrol enters what is known as the jet, or spraying nozzle, a thin vertical column of brass having a vertical central passage of very small diameter through which a fine stream of petrol rises and finally issues from the orifice in the form (as before said) of spray, to be mixed with air, and thus converted into the vapour known as petrol gas. The jet is screwed into position from the underside and is adapted, in the latest carburettors, so that it may be readily removed, or various other sizes substituted, without interfering with any other part.

The spraying chamber is provided underneath with apertures, through which a permanent supply of air can enter for mixing with the petrol spray as it rises from the jet orifice. This is called, for the sake of abbreviation, the " fixed " air intake.

It is obvious, however, that the main parts of the carburettor cannot be changed to suit different types and sizes of engines, so a little device known as the adapter, or choke-tube, is employed. The function of this is to shut off a certain percentage of the permanent air supply, and in this simple manner it is possible in a very short time to find the exact requirements of any particular engine.

The bore of the jet and the diameter of the adapter are calculated on the basis of the size and power of the engine to be fed. If the engine is large, a large size adapter is used, with a correspondingly large jet, the sizes varying proportionately. The adapter merely consists either of a piece of plain tubing formed of thin brass with a small flange at the top ; or it may have a truncated portion at the bottom to act as a funnel or intake for the air. In addition to the fixed air supply, means are provided for admitting to the spraying chamber a variable supplementary supply, this being called the "extra" air, and controlled by a valve or slide which may be adjusted to give any degree of opening that the circumstances call for by means of a small handle provided near the rider's hand for the purpose.

Carburation and Successful Working.

The whole secret of successful working in a petrol engine is to get the "mixture," as the gaseous fuel is generally called, correctly proportioned in respect of the percentages of petrol and air which combine to produce it. A weak mixture, *i.e.*, one into which air enters too largely, causes weak explosions, owing to the fact that the gas supplied to the cylinder lacks the substance required to produce the necessary force on being ignited, so that power is lost in driving the piston and the engine fails to perform the task required of it ; and if the mixture is *very* weak, it may be quite impossible to obtain explosion at all. On the other hand, if the gas is too rich—that is, without its proper admixture of air—a similar result will follow due to imperfect combustion, and, in any case, the rate of petrol consumption will be increased and overheating of the engine may ensue.

When the fuel delivered to the engine is correctly mixed, there is a wonderful difference in the working of the latter, and every motor cyclist should endeavour as much as possible, both in his own interests and that of the engine itself, to study this very important aspect of manipulating a petrol engine. The further remarks to be found in Chapter XII, which deals in part with the subject of driving a motor cycle, will, it is hoped, assist the reader in this direction.

The space above the jet forms a chamber in which the gas forms, and from whence it passes directly to the engine cylinder. Its upper cylindrical portion contains the air and throttle valves, or slides, by means of which the admission of the gas and the "extra" air are separately controlled. These valves are now-a-days operated from the handle-bar by means of Bowden cables, hence the term "handle-bar controlled" carburettor. They were formerly operated by small handles, attached to the sides of the petrol tank, which actuated rod and lever mechanism communicating with the carburettor, and this system one hears referred to as "tank control." It is now obsolete so far as modern construction is concerned.

Each valve or slide consists of a hollow body, of semicircular or **D**-shaped section, containing a spring which assists in controlling the movements of the valve. The outlet branch-piece (H), by means of which the carburettor is coupled up to the induction pipe of the engine, communicates with the interior of the spraying and valve chamber, which latter at its opposite side has an opening (I) for the admission of the supplementary air supply, this opening being controlled by the air valve operated by the rider (as before said) from the handle-bar. The float chamber is provided with a plunger (J) by means of which the float may be depressed, and the needle valve consequently raised and kept off its seating, so that the float is prevented from cutting off the petrol until the chamber is full.

FIG. 48.—The Latest "B. & B." Motor Cycle Carburettor.

This is what is known as "flooding" the carburettor, and it is usually resorted to prior to a start, so that the petrol may rise in the jet and the action of the carburettor be in part commenced while the engine is as yet stationary.

When the engine is working the petrol is drawn through the jet by the suction stroke of the piston, further assisted, maybe, by the current of air passing upward through the permanent openings in the base of the mixing chamber; and when the engine in the course of its working has depleted the supply in the float chamber, the float gradually descends and the needle valve opens to admit a fresh supply. Thus we have the following system of action :—

1. Petrol flows from tank through petrol pipe to the float chamber.

FIG. 49.—The Latest "B. & B." Carburettor, with Handle Bar Control Fittings.

2. Petrol enters the float chamber and raises the float until the balance weights reach a predetermined height, at which point the needle valve is forced

back into its seating and cuts off further ingress of petrol until the float is again allowed to descend as the engine consumes the petrol which is keeping it up. As the float descends so the balance weights also move with it, and the needle valve is again lifted to let in a further supply of petrol.

3. Petrol passes through small passage into the jet, and, so long as engine is working, is drawn through it by the suction of the engine, and being mixed with air, passes from the carburettor through the inlet pipe to the inlet valve chamber of engine and thence into the cylinder, in the form of a gaseous vapour of a highly explosive character.

The " B. & B." Carburettor.

The carburettor selected to illustrate the principle of carburation, as above described, is that known as the "B. & B.," manufactured by Messrs. Brown & Barlow, Ltd., of Holt Street, Birmingham. The author's long acquaintance with this make of carburettor has led him to form a very high opinion of its efficiency, and, in the latest patterns especially, everything possible has been done to ensure instant accessibility to every part, while the general construction is of the most simple character and the workmanship throughout of the highest class. The sectional view on page 64 shows the general construction of the carburettor. The needle valve is completely covered in and its seating is made separate from the body, and can therefore be readily replaced if desired. The spraying chamber is fixed to the float chamber by a special form of clip, the same arrangement being used for attaching the carburettor to the inlet pipe. By this method—to detach the float chamber from the spraying chamber—it is only requisite to unscrew the nut (K)—or, in the case of the 1911 pattern, the pin—half a turn, when the spraying chamber can be turned in any direction in relation to the float chamber, or completely withdrawn for inspection if desired. The same applies, as before said, to the fastening between the carburettor and the inlet pipe. Half a turn of the union nut (L) releases the carburettor, when it can be at once detached.

THE CARBURETTOR. 71

The jet is detached from underneath by simply unscrewing the small nut (M), when the jet can be withdrawn in less time than it takes to write it. The throttle and air valves, with all their parts, are made under Messrs. Brown & Barlow's patented bayonet joint, which renders them extremely easy of access. A quarter turn of the cap (N) allows the cap, complete with adjusting bushes, air and throttle valves, and all their parts to be withdrawn for inspection, when the adapter can be removed and, if desired, replaced by another one differing from it in size. Any one of the above operations can be effected without interfering with other parts of the carburettor. In the latest, or 1911, pattern (Figs. 48 and 49) "B. & B." carburettor (also illustrated) a hot-air intake funnel is attached to the lower portion of the spraying chamber, so that the possibility of freezing up the mixture during very cold weather may be avoided. This intake has a bell-shaped mouth, which is brought close to the engine cylinder to collect heat given off from the radiating fins. Vaporisation of the petrol is materially assisted by this device in cold atmospheres.

FIG. 50.
Removing Jet from " B. & B." Carburettor.

FIG. 50A. — Removing Air and Throttle Slides, "B. & B." Carburettor.

The author has found the " B. & B." carburettor extremely reliable, and to allow of wide variations of engine speeds, with economy at all stages. The handle-bar control mechanism gives no trouble whatever, and can be relied upon to perform its functions with accuracy for an indefinite period. The makers supply a small leather case containing four jets, varying in the size of the bore, and, as already explained, it is but a moment or two's work to change from one jet to another, should such a step appear desirable. The table given below sets out in convenient form the size of jet and adapter to go with it, recommended for given engine horsepower for ordinary touring service. This is largely departed from for special purposes, such as racing, hill-climbing, etc.

Bore of cylinder.	H.-P. of engine.	Size of jet.	Size of adapter.
64 mm.	2 h.-p.	·026 in.	·40 in.
70 mm.	2¾ ,,	·029 in.	·44 in.
76 mm.	3 ,,	·031 in.	·44 in.
86 mm.	3½ ,,	·032 in.	·53 in.
89 mm.	4 ,,	·033 in.	·56 in.

The " Amac " Carburettor.

Another well-known British carburettor is the " Amac," made by the Aston Motor Accessories Company, Ltd., of Birmingham. This carburettor shares with the " B. & B.",

FIG. 51.—Case Containing Four Jets of Different Bores for "B. & B." Carburettor.

previously described, the distinction of being fitted to the bulk of motor cycles manufactured in this country and to many of foreign origin also; indeed, it would hardly be going too far to say that 75 per cent. of modern motor cycles are fitted with either one or other of the carburettors named, the bulk of the British manufacturers giving their customers the option of having either the

THE CARBURETTOR.

FIG. 52.—Sectional Elevation of the "Amac" 1910 Carburettor.

" B. & B." or the "Amac," and, whichever way the point is decided, the purchaser cannot go far wrong.

The "Amac" carburettor, of which illustrations appear on this and the previous page, differs from the one previously described in several points of detail, and its outward appearance is also somewhat dissimilar. The spraying and valve

FIG. 53.—The "Amac" 1910 Carburettor, complete with Handle-Bar Control Fittings.

chambers are hemispherical in form and superimposed the one upon the other, the float chamber at the side being cylindrical in shape, as in the "B. & B." carburettor. The "Amac" needle valve, as seen, has a conical base tapering outwards towards the bottom, the seating being in this case inverted and so arranged that the valve moves upward to shut off the petrol instead of downward, as before. The cover (or cap) of the float chamber, instead of being screwed into place, is locked by means of a spring catch, and a single turn is sufficient to lift it off; and in this arrangement the level of the petrol in the jet is not affected by removing the cap. A gauze petrol filter is placed inside the union which connects the petrol pipe with the base of the float chamber. The jet (or nozzle) is held in position by means of a spring at the bottom of the carburettor, and to remove it the spring has to be compressed, and the piece which presses against the jet turned sideways, when the jet at once drops out.

Realising the necessity which sometimes arises for changing the size of the jet, so that a larger or smaller feed of petrol may be obtained at will, the "Amac" firm has made the jet adjustable in size. Instead of having the petrol regulating orifice at the top of the jet, they place six different sized holes at the bottom, all leading to the same central passage to supply the mixing chamber with petrol. Only one of these six holes is connected up at a time with the petrol supply to the float chamber, and by turning the small jet lever one is enabled, while riding, to obtain either a larger or smaller jet opening, as may have become necessary.

As before explained, a larger jet increases the power of the engine, but means a higher petrol consumption; while a smaller one, although slightly reducing the power, effects an economy in petrol, and it is a simple matter to ascertain which size of jet best suits the engine for the work it has to do. It is advantageous to bring a larger jet into use sometimes, temporarily, as when a big hill has to be climbed, or when for any other reason extra work is thrown upon the engine, and then, when the conditions again become easier, the smaller jet may be reverted to. By making the jet with six openings a good range of settings can be obtained; but it must be explained that only three can be used in running, and it is for the individual rider to choose which three are most suitable. The amount of petrol which issues from the large opening at the top is dependent on the amount admitted at the bottom, and the size of the jet orifice is approximately the same as in the single jet carburettor, so that the usual trouble experienced with multiple jet carburettors—*i.e.*, stopped up passages, is overcome.

76 THE MOTOR CYCLIST'S HANDBOOK.

The "Amac" jet is designed with a tube up the centre, allowing air to enter the carburettor through it, and, by this means, it is claimed that instead of the petrol entering as one solid stream, it does so in the form of a hollow column, with an air cone in it. This air cone strikes against the tapered base of the throttle valve and sprays the air all round the valve, thus assisting to obtain a much improved mixture.

The mixing chamber is fitted with a hot-air inlet as in the case of the 1911 pattern "B. & B." carburettor previously described. This hot-air inlet is arranged to swing in

Fig. 54.—The Latest "Amac" Carburettor for Motor Cycle Engines.

any direction, so that when not required, as during warm or normal weather, it may be swung away from the engine. The throttle and extra air valves take the form of piston valves fitted with rings to ensure a good fit and to obviate the difficulty sometimes experienced through valves sticking. The valves are operated by levers on the handle-bar through Bowden (protected) cables. The air and throttle levers are moved in the same direction; they work in a horizontal plane and are fitted with ebonite handles. The drawings and other illustrations of the two carburettors selected for special description, together with the explanations by which

THE CARBURETTOR.

they are accompanied, will, it is hoped, serve to make quite clear to the beginner—and also perhaps to those claiming to be more experienced—the features of construction and working employed by two of the leading British carburettor manufacturers. It will be gathered that everything is done to simplify the construction and to facilitate the handling of what is generally acknowledged to be one of the most important adjuncts of a motor cycle engine. The latest, or 1911 "Amac" carburettor has a cylindrical spraying chamber in which are arranged five spraying orifices with air channels between them.

FIG. 55.—The New "Amac" Carburettor, complete with Handle-Bar Control Fittings.

These five orifices are in direct communication with a small chamber to which petrol is delivered by the actual jet below them. The throttle and air valves are flat and bevelled down at the bottom to fit down upon the body of the five supplementary jets. The air valve has pieces cut out at the sides to allow of air being admitted under all conditions of running. Air also enters through the base of the spraying chamber and passes upwards between the five secondary jets.

Other Well-known Carburettors

fitted to motor cycles include the "F.N.", "Longuemare," and "J.A.P." The last-named is a good example of construction on the automatic principle. It is divided into eight sections. There are eight air passages (A), through the main casting (B), each air passage having its own petrol supply. Each section is closed or opened one after the other, as desired, by the throttle (C). It is obvious that the air and petrol are therefore supplied or cut off by the throttle (C) in exact proportion.

FIG. 56.—The "J.A.P." Automatic Carburettor.

The float chamber is of usual construction, and supplies petrol at a uniform level to chamber (D), in which is secured the fine gauze strainer (F), through which the petrol is strained immediately before passing through the jet supply passages (G). The jets are formed by grooves cut in the under face of the jet plate (H), this being secured by screw (E). The throttle cap (K) is secured by four screws and nuts of special form, which fit into slots allowing them to be easily removed. The jet plate (H) can then be readily inspected.

The automatic extra air inlet consists of a perforated plate, fixed between the flanges of the throttle cap (K) and the jet chamber (B) (the plate is not shown in the sectional drawing).

This plate is provided with extra air inlets, one to each air hole (A), with the exception of the hole first opened by the throttle. These extra air holes are closed by balls of phosphor-bronze, which lift off their seatings and let in the extra air, when the suction on the jet exceeds a certain amount. The mixing process is thus rendered rather more simple by arranging that the proportion of air required to suit a given throttle opening is adjusted automatically, so that the rider, instead of having to judge, or find by means of varying the position of the extra air lever, how much supplementary air the engine will take at different throttle openings, has it done for him, there being in this case only one operating lever, which controls both the throttle and the air supply. Whether the adjustments are capable of such refinement with this method as when each controlling valve is separately and independently controlled, may seem open to question; but

FIG. 57.—Sectional View of " J.A.P." Automatic Carburettor.

it is certainly the fact, that "automatic" carburettors are successfully used and are identified with some of the most remarkable performances ever attributed to a motor cycle. For every-day touring the author would personally prefer the separate method of control; but this remark must not be construed into one of prejudice against the automatic system.

The Longuemare carburettor—a French make—has a great reputation, and was in the earlier days of the motor cycle movement in this country almost exclusively employed.

It is still held in high favour, and deservedly so ; but the average rider of experience now looks upon it rather as an old and respected friend than as the companion of his present-day motor cycling experiences. The Longuemare apparatus has been much improved of late, and anyone preferring it will be quite safe in stipulating for its attachment to his machine.

Carburettor Adjustments and Control.

Regarding the broad subject of carburation in relation to the motor cycle engine, there are many points associated with the adjustment and control of the apparatus which require attention. In reality the adjustments are few but *very*

FIG. 58.—The Longuemare Motor Cycle Carburettor.

important, and, once having got them right, the old advice as to " letting well alone " cannot be too closely adhered to. The process of " tuning up " a carburettor does not, as some seem to think, follow a stated rule ; but depends very largely upon individual circumstances connected with the type and working conditions of the particular engine ; but it must not, on the other hand, be supposed that one has to go groping about altogether in the dark as to what is wrong before being able to effect any improvement.

THE CARBURETTOR.

There *is* a process or system of adjustment based upon the symptoms displayed by the engine when working irregularly, and if these symptoms are traced beyond doubt to trouble with the carburettor, then a predetermined plan can be put into execution which must very soon elucidate the precise cause of the trouble and put it right.

When the engine shows a falling off of power, or refuses to start easily, the average rider says " carburettor " at once, and proceeds to alter the petrol level in the jet, change the jet itself for another size, or otherwise tamper with the existing adjustments ; but too much stress *cannot* be laid on the point that unless the symptoms are so pronounced, or something about the carburettor itself shows distinctly that it is indeed a fault connected with the mixing or feed of the vapour, the motor cyclist should first ascertain that it is not the charge but the means of igniting it that is wrong. In other words, let him first see that he is getting an efficient spark wherewith to explode the mixture before he does anything in the way of trying to " improve " the apparatus which produces it ; and, further, he must also make sure that the valves of his engine are working properly, admitting and expelling the charge, before tackling the question of faulty carburation.

The explanation of the methods usually resorted to in adjusting the carburettor is reserved until the Chapter on Overhauling and Tuning up the Engine is reached, the author's purpose being that the main points connected with the adjustment and control of the engine and its principal component parts may be followed in sequence and by reading consecutive pages, and that the more detailed information bearing upon these points should be reserved until after the reader has made himself acquainted with the name and purposes of the different parts constituting every branch of the construction.

CHAPTER VII.

THE IGNITION.

THE apparatus employed for igniting the explosive mixture in a motor cycle engine is possibly less well understood by the majority of riders than any other part of the construction. They regard it as something in the nature of a mystery, and one often hears the remark, " I'm no good at electricity," made by the motor cyclist whose engine is suffering from some complaint connected with the ignition. The author well realises that the beginner is placed at a considerable disadvantage unless he possesses an average knowledge of electrical matters, and would suggest that he carefully peruses the general explanations which follow as to the methods of producing the electric spark and the appliances by means of which it is caused, to effect the purpose of igniting the charge within the cylinder.

Evolution of Ignition Methods.

Amongst the earliest forms of ignition to be used in a gas engine—which is similar in principle to a petrol engine—was the electric spark. This form of ignition has exceptional advantages ; but, at first, it was found impossible to make it reliable, and, as a consequence, the electric-spark principle gave way to flame ignition, and then to red-hot metal surface ignition, the commonest form of which is a red-hot tube, into which the gas is compressed when ignition is required. In a gas or petrol engine there is a very brief moment in which the gas should be ignited, if good results are to be obtained from the engine. Even in a slow-running gas engine it is not possible to make the ignition occur very accurately with the flame or hot-tube method, and in a petrol engine, as applied to motor cycles, the accuracy of ignition at exactly the right moment is of far greater importance, owing to the high speed at which the engine runs.

Now the electric spark can be made to occur at absolutely the correct moment, and it is chiefly for this reason that this form of ignition is practically universal on all petrol engines at the present day. Even in the early days, when any trouble occurred with such engines, it was generally safe to assume that the ignition was the cause ; but the subject has received such a great amount of very skilled attention since, that the ignition apparatus is now fully as reliable as any part of the motor cycle.

Production of the Electric Spark.

There are several forms of electric ignition in use on motor cycle engines, but each system has the same essential parts, consisting as follows :—

(1) An instrument for producing an electric spark;
(2) A prepared path for the spark to travel from the instrument producing it to the fitting on the engine where it is required ; and,
(3) An appliance on the engine at which the spark occurs.

Instruments for producing the electric spark can be divided into two main classes, viz.—the coil and battery system, and the magneto system. The coil and battery system consists of a battery in which a low-pressure electric current is chemically stored, and a coil, which is an instrument for converting the low-pressure current from the battery into a high-pressure current or electric spark. There is required, in addition, a mechanical device, driven by the engine, to decide when the spark shall occur, this fitting being called a contact-maker, contact-breaker, or wipe contact, according to the various forms in which it is made. The magneto system may be said to combine the above three parts in one.

The next point to be considered is the prepared path for the spark to travel between the magneto or coil to the engine, and this is called the high-tension cable. It is convenient to think of the spark travelling down this cable, although in reality it is an electric current of small quantity, but of very high electrical pressure or tension. It has been found that an electric current will flow very easily in all metals, and only with great difficulty in such materials as rubber, porcelain, mica, or ebonite, and many others, and these last named are called insulators.

Dry air is a good insulator, and it requires a high electrical pressure to jump across even quite a small air-gap.

compressed air is a still more powerful insulator. The high-tension cable consists of several strands of copper wire twisted together, which are completely enclosed in a thick covering of rubber.

The fitting on the engine at which the electric spark occurs is called a sparking plug, and it consists simply of a short thick wire, carefully insulated from the engine. One end of the wire is outside the engine, and is arranged with a suitable fitting for connecting it with the high-tension cable. The other end is inside the engine, and so arranged that there is a very small air-space between this wire and another one, also forming a part of the plug, and which is touching the inside metal of the engine. These two are commonly referred to as the sparking plug " points," and across the small gap by which they are separated the high-tension current has to jump. In doing so, it makes the air or gas in its path white-hot, and so produces ignition of the gaseous mixture within the cylinder.

Ignition Apparatus : Dry Battery System.

We may next turn our attention to the form and application of the different kinds of apparatus employed to convey the principle of ignition to its practical uses.

FIG. 59.—The " Hellesen " Dry Battery.

In the coil-and-battery system the battery forms a very convenient method of supplying a portable means of producing the electric spark. Batteries are divided into two main classes, called primary and secondary. Dry batteries (a form of primary cell) produce an electrical current by chemical action, and when all the current that they will give has been

THE IGNITION.

taken out of them they are of no further use for ignition, but may be employed for electric bells, telephones, etc., and will give long service thereon.

A primary battery generates an electric current by chemical action between the elements which constitute the battery.

The only primary battery suitable for motor ignition is the dry battery, a diagram of which is shown. It is made up with a zinc outer case, which is insulated on the outside by means of a cardboard case impregnated with insulating material, and in the centre of the zinc case is placed a carbon block, which forms the positive (+) pole of the cell, whilst the terminal attached to the outer zinc forms the negative (−) pole. Surrounding the carbon block is packed a mixture consisting of broken carbon, graphite, and manganese di-oxide ; this composition is tightly compressed round the carbon rod, and is held in position by a cloth sack, the space between this sack and the zinc case is filled in with a thick paste of jelly, which forms the active material or electrolyte ; above the sack a separate compartment is arranged, which is filled with husks, or similar material, so as to form a receptacle for any gas which may be formed during the time the cell is in action ; the upper portion of this compartment is formed by a special layer of asphalt, through which a small glass vent tube projects into the husks, so as to allow the gas to escape.

FIG. 60.—External View of the "Hellesen" Dry Battery.

Dry batteries have the advantage of convenience, due to the fact that there is no acid to spill, no charging to look after, and no corroded terminals, and also to the fact that they are always ready for immediate use without any attention whatever.

The above is a general description of the well-known " H. H." Hellesen dry battery, for which it is claimed it does not deteriorate when not in actual use, so that the mileage can be taken from it over extended periods, thus rendering it exceptionally suitable for use on motor-cars, cycles, and motor boats generally.

Accumulators and Coils.

The secondary battery does not actually produce a current, but can store it and give it out when required. Despite the fact that these batteries (or accumulators, as they are generally termed) are made with heavy lead plates, and have to contain dilute sulphuric acid, they are quite the most common form in use, on account of the the large current that can be stored, and the fact that they can be used over and over again by re-charging, which, in other words, means simply passing an electrical current into them.

Fig. 60A.—Diagram of Wiring for Accumulator Ignition.

(A)—Accumulator. (B)—Coil. (C)—Sparkling Plug. (D)—Contact Breaker. (E)—Interrupter Plug. (F)—Switch.

Batteries or accumulators, as arranged for motor cycle work, have two terminals, to which the high-tension wires are connected. One of these terminals is called the positive terminal, and is usually either painted red or marked with a plus (+); while the other is called the negative terminal, and is painted black or marked with a negative sign (−). It is of the greatest importance that these two terminals be never joined together by metal or wire, as this "short-circuits" the battery and does great harm.

Fig. 61.—Accumulator for Motor Cycle Use.

Coils are instruments used to transform the low-pressure battery current to a high enough pressure to jump the spark-gap at the sparking plug. A coil consists of a soft-iron core, round which are wound two layers of thick copper wire, outside which are a very large number of turns of very thin

THE IGNITION.

wire, and to produce the spark the battery current is sent round the thick-wire coil and suddenly interrupted. The coils are made up in two chief forms—*i.e.*, plain (or non-trembler) coils, and trembler coils. In a non-trembler or plain coil the sudden stoppage of the battery current is performed by a mechanical device on the engine called the contact-breaker. This contact-breaker makes contact for a moment, and then suddenly breaks contact at the correct moment when the spark is required.

FIG. 62.—Adjusting Mechanism of Trembler Coil.

In a trembler coil the sudden stoppage is performed by a magnetic device on the coil itself, similar to an electric bell, and called the trembler. These coils work with a contact-maker or wipe contact, this fitting making the contact and so allowing the current to pass to the coil at the moment when the spark is required to ignite the explosive charge in the cylinder.

FIG. 62A.—Contact-breaker with Single Blade for Single-cylinder Engine.

Coils usually have three or four terminals, to which wires have to be connected. Two of these terminals are always low-tension, and one high-tension, except when there are four terminals, and then there are two high-tension.

This number of terminals applies to single coils for single-cylinder engines. The terminals are either labelled or have letters to show what part of the ignition apparatus they are to connect up with by means of the wires.

On an English coil these letters are usually :—

C = Contact Maker.
B (or A) = Battery or Accumulator.
P (or SP) = Plug or Sparking Plug.
E (or F) = Earth or Frame.

French coils usually have the following letters :—

C = Contact Maker.
P = Pile = Battery.
B = Bougie = Sparking Plug.
M = Masse = Earth.

FIG. 62B.—Contact-breaker with Double Blades for Twin-cylinder Engine.

The Magneto System.

The magneto is an instrument which generates a low-tension current mechanically. This current is suddenly interrupted in a manner quite similar in principle to the ignition coil; but there is no battery, and the contact-breaker is combined with the instrument itself. The magneto system requires very little wiring, and very little attention is required to keep it in order. It is universally applied to modern motor cycles, for which purpose it is far and away the most suitable which can be devised.

The current can only be generated while the engine is in motion, and that, of course, is the only time when it is really needed. When the engine stops the magneto machine stops working also, as it derives its motion by means of a

THE IGNITION. 89

chain or gear drive from the engine itself, which rotates the armature shaft and sets the system in motion which results in producing the electric spark to ignite the explosive charge.

The diagrams (Fig. 63, 1-3), in conjunction with the remarks accompanying them, provide an easy method of studying the action of the magneto.

Fig. 1 shows the path of the magnetic lines due to the field, with the armature in the position shown, and with the low-pressure or primary winding on open circuit. It will be noticed that all the lines pass through the core of the armature, as is natural, owing to the lines much preferring an iron path to an air path. The lines, in passing through the core, also thread through every turn of wire on the armature.

Fig. 2 shows the path of the magnetic lines when the armature has turned through 90 degs. All the magnetic lines now

(N)—North Pole.   (S)—South Pole.

Fig. 63.—Showing the Action of the Magneto and Path of the Magneto Lines.

pass through the ends of the armature, but to get to this position they have had to cut every turn in the armature winding. If the winding had been a closed circuit, a current would have been produced in the winding, the amount of the current being dependent on the resistance of the turns and the pressure developed. The pressure produced depends on the strength of the magnetic field, the number of turns in the armature primary winding, and the rate at which the magnetic lines are cut by the winding, or, in other words, the speed of the armature.

When the armature has revolved through another 90 degs., the path of the magnetic lines is as shown in Fig. 1 again; but, as the field is always in one direction, it will be observed that the lines pass through the winding in the reverse direction. For this reason, when two sparks are produced in each revolution, the sparks will be in alternate directions.

It should be clearly understood that the above diagrams only show the path of the magnetic lines on an open armature circuit. If the winding is closed and the armature revolving, the current is produced in the winding, the greatest current being when the armature is in *about* the position shown in Fig. 2. But this current round the armature core produces a magnetic field of its own. This armature magnetic field distorts the permanent magnetic field in the direction of rotation, and makes the point of strongest armature current, and therefore strongest armature field, later than shown in Fig. 2.

It is this distortion of the magnetic field that makes the design of the advance and retard of magneto ignition so awkward. Much the simplest and neatest form of timing the ignition is to revolve the contact-breaking points through a small angle, so that they either separate a little earlier or later than usual. As the position where it is suitable to break the current extends over a very small angle, and as the distortion of the field occurs in the same direction as the rotation, while to advance the ignition the contact points have to be revolved against the direction of rotation, it will be appreciated that the range of movement is still further limited. The result in practice is that, for starting, the break has to occur in rather a bad position ; and, owing to the speed of the armature being slow at starting, it explains that it is sometimes necessary to advance the spark, even for starting, in order to get a good enough firing spark. It is for the above reason that many machines have the timing of the ignition fixed.

Fig. 3 shows the magnetic field with the armature primary winding closed, and revolving at a good speed, the armature being in the position just before the contact points are going to separate. The lines of force of the permanent magnetic field are shown by dotted lines, and the lines due to the armature current are shown in full.

It will be seen that the armature field opposes the permanent magnet field, and this explains the de-magnetising effect that occurs if the armature is short-circuited by means of a switch, so as to use the engine as a brake. There is probably no harm in switching off the magneto in this way, but the magneto should not be driven at a high speed as when coasting down a long hill with the armature short-circuited. If, however, the makers of magnetos arranged so that the switch left the armature circuit open, there would be no harm in using the engine as a brake. As it is, the Bosch Magneto Company claims there is no risk and that the life of the magneto is not appreciably decreased by the use of the switch, or, as it is commonly called, the magneto "cut-out," an illustration of which, attached to the handlebar of a motor bicycle is given in Fig. 63A.

From an examination of this diagram, the quick reversion in the armature field that takes place as soon as the contact points are separated will easily be understood. As soon as the contact points separate, the current in the armature

Fig. 63A.—Handle-Bar Cut-out Switch; Magneto Ignition.

circuit is stopped, and there is nothing to sustain the armature field, and therefore the permanent magnetic field, which it has been opposing, at once overpowers it, thus causing exceedingly quick reversal of the magnetism, and inducing a very powerful spark.

The power taken to drive a single-cylinder magneto is about $\frac{1}{15}$ h.-p. at normal maximum speeds. The power required increases roughly as the square of the speed; but not exactly, owing to distortion of the field.

In a single-cylinder magneto there are two maximum positions; but only one position is used, as the armature is kept on open circuit by the platinum points being kept apart as the armature revolves through this position.

In the case of two-cylinder V engines the correct timing is obtained by making specially shaped pole-pieces and a specially shaped armature, as indicated in Fig. 64. The

Fig. 64.—Armature and Pole-Pieces for V Type Twin-cylinder Engines.

effect of this arrangement is to make the two maximum positions occur at the correct angle for firing each cylinder, instead of being exactly opposite, as they would be with a normal magneto.

Construction and Working of the Bosch Magneto.

Passing on from this to a consideration of the detailed construction of the magneto and the functions of the various parts

Fig. 65.—Diagram showing Wiring Connections, Bosch High-tension Magneto Ignition.

the diagram (Fig. 65), for the use of which the author is indebted to the Bosch Magneto Company, Ltd., clearly shows the wiring and points connected with the magneto system

THE IGNITION.

of ignition, and the details of the apparatus can be followed by referring to the other illustrations.

The principle of operation is as follows: Between the pole shoes of two steel magnets which form a strong magnetic field, a so-called shuttle armature rotates, and by reason of this motion a current is produced in the armature winding, which reaches its maximum twice in one revolution, but one of which is used only for effecting a spark between the electrodes or points of the sparking plug. The jumping of the spark across this air-gap has already been explained. The armature is built up of thin sheets of metal securely held together, and is wound in two parts—one forming a continuation of the other, and of which the inner winding (C^1) is the primary, consisting of a few turns of heavy wire ; and the other, the secondary (C^2), consisting of many turns of fine wire. The electrical current is produced in the primary winding by the rotation of the armature, and, by the interruption of the primary circuit by means of a contact-breaker, a high-tension current is induced in the secondary winding, which at the moment of the separating or breaking, as it is termed, of the contact point causes a spark to jump across the electrodes of the sparking plug and fires the charge within the cylinder of the engine.

As the arc-like spark can only be produced when the armature is in a certain position, and as the ignition has to take place at a certain period in the movement of the piston, it becomes necessary that the armature shall be positively driven at the same speed as the cam-shaft of the engine. To effect this a chain or gear-wheel is affixed to the end of the cam shaft of the engine, and another chain or gear-wheel—of the same diameter and pitch exactly—to the end of the magneto armature shaft, and the two are connected up, either by a chain or intermediate gear-wheels, as the case may be, so that the armature shaft is bound to rotate at the same speed as the cam shaft.

This gearing is shortly referred to as the " magneto drive," and is enclosed within an aluminium casing to protect it from dust and dirt.

The variation of the moment at which the spark shall occur within the cylinder, in accordance with the position of the piston working therein, is effected on the magneto itself by means of the timing lever, causing the interruption of the primary current to take place earlier or later in relation to the stroke of the piston.

This is called the timing of the spark, and it exercises a very considerable influence on the working of the engine. A lever or small handle—termed the firing or spark lever— is affixed to the tank or handle-bar of the motor bicycle, and this connects with the contact-breaker by means of a rod or Bowden wire attached to a short arm on the steel segment, which influences the making and breaking of the contact points. The precise manner in which the various parts work, and the part each plays in producing the electric spark and controlling the periods of its occurrence, may be best described as follows. Referring to the drawings, Figs. 66 and 67, in conjunction with one another :—

The contact-breaker disc (5) rotates with the armature, and is directly coupled to it ; but is detachable, and held by means of the screw (9) into the rear end of the armature spindle, which is bored to receive it. The contact-breaker disc (5) is prevented from rotating in the bored end of the spindle by means of a key and keyway, which also make it impossible to place the contact-breaker in a wrong position. On the disc (5) the bell-crank lever (6) is fitted, carrying at one end a small platinum point, attached by means of a nut and screwed portion, and at the other extremity a fibre segment projecting laterally. The platinum screw on the bell-crank lever aforesaid is pressed against a similar platinum screw on the contact-piece (8) by means of a spring (7). The contact-piece (8) is fastened to the contact-breaker disc (5), but is insulated therefrom, and is electrically connected by the screw (9) to the contact-plate (1), and consequently with the end of the primary winding.

The screw (9), which holds the complete contact-breaker in position, enables it to be readily removed for the purpose of cleaning the platinum points, and this method of construction facilitates the removal of worn or damaged parts and the replacement of the same.

We now come to the timing lever, to which reference has already been made. The timing lever (10) is held on to the end plate of the magneto by means of a shoulder turned thereon, so that it can rotate through a certain distance, to effect an advance and retard in the moment of firing. Attached to the timing lever (10) is the steel segment (11),

THE IGNITION.

and inside this slip-ring the contact-breaker revolves. The parts (10) and (11)—that is, the timing lever and steel cam—form one piece with a brass ring, and the whole can be rotated, within certain limits, around the contact-breaker, whether the latter is stationary or in motion, so altering the moment in the process of rotation at which the bell-crank lever comes in contact with the steel segment, and thus causing the spark to take place earlier or later in the stroke of the piston, as may be desired.

The bell-crank lever (6) is connected through the contact-breaker disc (5) with the armature spindle, the armature core, and one end of the primary winding; whilst the contact-piece (8) is connected with its other end, and when the fibre head of the bell-crank lever reaches the steel segment, the lever (6) is deflected, and the primary circuit broken by separation of the two platinum points. If, when the interruption of the circuit occurs, the armature is in a suitable position, the voltage of the current induced in the secondary winding will be sufficiently high to cause a very intense spark to pass between the points of the sparking plug.

The Condenser.

Other parts of the construction shown in the drawings, Figs. 66 and 67, include the condenser (17), the function of which is to prevent the arc due to the current induced in the winding by the collapse of the armature field. The condenser is connected across the two contact-breaking points and consists of a number of thin metal plates separated by paraffin paper or mica. Every alternate metal plate is electrically connected to another, and the set of alternate plates to one platinum point.

Fig. 66.—Section through Armature and Contact-Breaker of Bosch Single-cylinder Magneto.

The other set of plates are electrically connected to the remaining platinum point.

The condenser, after charging, discharges itself into the low-tension winding, causing the magnetic field to collapse exceedingly quickly. The current from the discharge of the condenser being in the reverse direction, a magnetic field is developed in opposition to the previous field.

Collection and Distribution of the Current.

The slip ring with distributing segment (2) provides a means of distributing the high-tension current generated by the magneto to a collector or carbon holder (4), this part consisting of a small brass tube with a solid portion at the top, above this being a brass knob on to which one end of the high-tension cable is " snapped " in a manner rather similar to a glove fastener. The little brass tube contains a small coil spring into which is inserted a rod or stick of carbon. This rod of carbon (or carbon brush, as it is called) is in contact with the distributor segment (2), being kept up to its work by the little aforementioned spring. The electrical current thus passes through the carbon holder to the cable, and by this means to the sparking plug. In the latest Bosch motor cycle magnetos for single-cylinder engines, as shown in Fig. 66, the snap terminal has been discarded and a watertight terminal with plunger cable connection (as illustrated) is fitted instead. The snap terminals are still being used on twin-cylinder magnetos, and all machines are being fitted with felt padding underneath the armature dust cover in order to render them entirely weather-proof. So far as the generation of current is concerned, it is immaterial which way the armature revolves, this point depending upon circumstances associated with the precise method of driving the magneto from the engine.

FIG. 67.—End View of Bosch Magneto with Contact-Breaker Cover Removed.

THE IGNITION. 97

The screw (12) is provided so that a length of low-tension insulated wiring may be led from the magneto to a switch on the handle-bar of the machine, so that the current may, if desired, be diverted from the sparking plug while the magneto is working. This forms an additional means of controlling and cooling the engine. The contact-breaker mechanism is protected by a dust-proof cover (14) held in place by the spring (15), which latter is turned sideways when it is desired to remove the cover for the purpose of inspecting the contact-breaker parts. Oil wells are provided on each side of the magneto to permit of the armature bearings being lubricated, this being only

FIG. 68.—External View of Bosch single-cylinder High-tension Magneto.

FIG. 69.—Bosch Magneto for Twin-cylinder Engine.

required at the rate of a few drops once a month with a ball-bearing magneto. By this time the reader will probably have gained a fair idea as to the manner in which the electric spark is produced, and by what means it is conveyed to the interior of the cylinder for igniting the charge, and will be wanting to know something of the precise method in which variation in the moment of sparking is effected and the result which such variation has on the working of the engine.

The Timing of the Spark while Riding.

As before said, there is provided for the riders' use on the tank of the motor cycle a small handle, attached to which is a rod, which, at its lower end, connects with the arm or timing lever (6) on the slip ring, which carries the steel segment (11), and which may be moved within certain limits around the contact-breaker. It has also been explained that the movement of the slip ring alters the relative positions of the steel segment and the fibre block on the end of the bell-crank lever, so that the two come in contact with one another either earlier or later in the path described by the contact-breaker points in rotating.

FIG. 70.—Contact-breaker with Double Segments for Twin-cylinder Engine.

FIG. 71.—Collector Ring and Carbon Brushes for Twin-cylinder Magneto.

As the coming in contact of these two parts effects the separation of the platinum points (thus interrupting the circuit and causing the spark to take place), it will be seen that as the moment of separation is varied so must the moment of sparking be also varied ; and, as the armature of the magneto is caused to rotate at the same speed as the engine camshaft, it naturally follows that the piston in the cylinder will have assumed a different position by the time any fresh adjustment of the timing lever has been made, so that the explosion occurs at an earlier or a later period in the piston stroke, according to whether the timing is advanced or retarded.

THE IGNITION.

FIG. 72.—Method of Timing the Ignition (Magneto System).

The variation of the movement is, of course, somewhat limited, matters being so devised that timing lever (10) carrying the steel segment (11) can be rotated through an angle not exceeding 35 degs., which is equal to a variation of 70 degs. on the engine.

Now, as to the purpose and effect of varying the moment of sparking. It might be supposed that the precise and only moment at which the mixture or gaseous charge ought to be exploded within the cylinder would be when the piston arrives at the end of its upward (compression) stroke and when the point of highest compression has thus been reached, so that as powerful an explosion as possible might result. If this condition were to be regarded as correct, and desirable under every condition of working, then there would be no need to provide any means of varying the sparking moment; and, indeed, a few makers *have* arranged their engines with fixed ignition and the rider has no means of altering it at his disposal. This method, like automatic carburation, may be desirable with some engines, but it is certainly not in the majority; and, speaking personally, the author much prefers to have both the ignition and carbureting arrangements designed for variation at will.

FIG. 72A.—A Piece of Wire, Bent and Passed through the Compression Tap, Locates the Position of the Piston.

Let us assume that the piston having drawn in the charge of mixture is moving upwards on the compression stroke. The gases are most highly compressed when the piston reaches the highest point of its travel, but it is not desirable to leave the moment of sparking until then, for there must be an appreciable, though very minute lapse of time between the moment at which the platinum points separate at the contact-breaker, the spark is produced at the sparking plug points, and the explosion of the gases actually takes place; so that if the spark is timed to occur slightly *before* the piston reaches the end of its upward stroke a complete combustion of the charge is effected and the force of the explosion is exerted at the most favourable moment for driving the engine at high speed.

So far we have only considered the timing of the spark as effected by the rider within the limits permitted by the tank control handle. There is another and even more important aspect of the matter.

The Permanent Setting of the Ignition.

As explained, every motor cycle engine fitted with magneto ignition is arranged so that the armature, and with it the contact-breaker, rotate in a certain co-relation to the movements of the piston, and this is effected by adjusting the chain or gear-wheels which serve to convey motion from the engine to the armature. The platinum points of the contact-breaker are set to break contact with one another just as the piston reaches the top of the compression stroke; this setting, however, being subject to the rider's manipulation of the handle, as before explained. It is an easy matter to adjust the timing of a magneto. First of all, the thing is to place the piston at the top of the compression stroke— that is to say, when it returns to the top of the cylinder and *both* valves are closed, keep it in that position; then rotate the contact-breaker by hand until the points are just on the point of separating, and with these two positions assured the gear or chain drive can be connected up. Before attempting to do anything with the other parts, however, place the firing handle on the tank at two-thirds retard position (Fig. 72) (with some engines it is possible to nearly fully retard the handle), and, of course, the more retard given at this juncture the earlier will the spark take place in the compression stroke when the handle is fully advanced, because of the wider range of advance movement afforded. If the spark is caused to take place too early in the compression stroke—that is to say, while the piston is too far off the end of its upward travel—the effect is to produce an explosion some time before the motion of the piston can be reversed, so that we have the piston being forced upward by the flywheels and connecting-rod, while the explosion at the same time is trying to force it downwards; it is, in other words,

Fig. 73.—The Meaning of a "Backfire."

THE IGNITION.

caught between two opposing forces, and this, as before pointed out, leads to what is termed "knocking" in the engine bearings, due to the jarring effect of what we may perhaps best call a collision between the opposing forces in the cylinder, and which jarring is conveyed downwards by means of the connecting-rod. This knocking occurs at low engine speeds with spark lever much advanced; and is undesirable enough, but an even worse evil, *i.e.*, what is termed "backfiring," may occur at *starting* when the ignition is much too far advanced. In the event of a severe back-fire taking place it is quite possible that serious damage may result to the connecting-rod, timing gears, or other part of the mechanism. The effect of the premature explosion is to suddenly and forcibly reverse the direction in which the flywheels are rotating, and the piston is subjected to a violent blow while still travelling upwards. Pre-ignition, or firing of the charge before the spark is timed to occur, may be brought about by the presence of heavy carbonised deposits, which under certain circumstances may assume an incandescent state of heat or a small projection or irregularity in the cylinder casting may in like circumstances effect the same result. The accompanying diagram, Fig. 73, shows clearly what takes place when a back-fire occurs.

If, on the other hand, the timing of the spark is too far delayed, or retarded, the explosion occurs when the piston has performed a material portion of the downward working stroke, so that before complete combustion is effected and the full force of the explosion is spent, the exhaust valve opens, the piston rises on the exhaust stroke, and the gases are expelled while still containing a lot of driving power. Loss of power and overheating of the engine follow, and the engine speed falls below what it should be. It is, therefore, necessary to manipulate the firing lever so that it is fully advanced, or very nearly so, for fast running, when the machine is well under way, and can be allowed to go along at a good rate of speed, and to slightly retard the timing for starting or when otherwise it is either obligatory or necessary to materially reduce the speed of the engine for some time.

So that what it amounts to is this : At starting, and when it is desired to run slowly, slightly retard the timing lever ; and when speed has been gathered, fully advance the spark and keep it there, so that full advantage may be taken of the force of explosion in driving the engine, only altering the position of the timing lever to one of more or less retard when circumstances call for it. Chapter XII, containing some hints on driving, will further emphasise these points.

When setting the ignition with a magneto, either one of two plans may be employed. In the case of a chain drive, the chain can be removed altogether and coupled up in place after the sprocket on the engine and that on the armature shaft have been got into the right positions, relatively to one another, or the sprocket on the armature shaft may be loosened without interfering with the chain itself, and the shaft revolved to get the right position ; the chain wheel being then locked on the shaft.

In a gear drive the intermediate gear-wheel (or wheels) may be taken out, and then, when the correct positions of the engine and magneto parts have been obtained, these gears replaced ; or, as before, the gear-wheel on end of armature shaft can be slackened off and afterwards tightened up again when all is correctly positioned. This last-named method permits of more minute and accurate adjustments being made as it is not dependent in any way upon the " pitch " of the teeth.

In the case of a twin-cylinder engine, the contact-breaker is fitted with two steel segments, one for each of the two cylinders, so that as the contact-breaker rotates the bell-crank lever twice comes in contact with a steel segment during every revolution, and the platinum points consequently break contact twice, at set (but not regular) intervals, except where the engine is designed on the principle of that described on pages 39 and 40, causing an electric spark to occur in each cylinder in turn every time the contact-breaker performs a complete revolution. In timing the ignition of a twin engine, it is only necessary to employ the same means as in a single cylinder one, the rear cylinder being usually selected for the purpose. Then when all is coupled up it will be found that if the timing is correct as set for the rear cylinder it is correct for the front one as well.

In order that the part of our subject now under consideration may be the better understood, it may be well at this point to make a few general remarks upon

The Theory of Ignition.

It is well to get a clear idea of what actually goes on in the cylinder after compression. The usual plan is to ignite the gas at one point, and from this point combustion spreads comparatively slowly at first, with increasing rapidity as the unburnt gas becomes heated up, and more highly compressed, and also as the surface of the igniting wave increases. The early stages of ignition are slow, because the igniting surface is exceedingly small; the initial stages are quicker with a large spark, which has a large igniting surface, and quicker still when two simultaneous sparks are used. The point at which ignition is started is also of considerable importance. This position should be chosen so that a good mixture is ensured in the neighbourhood of the sparking points, and the gas should be ignited as far away as possible from cold metal surfaces. With the above conditions fulfilled, and when the gas is ignited at one point, certainly the best position is in the centre of the compressed gas. Of course, a gas might be chosen, and such igniting arrangements made, that the expansion of the gas would be too sudden for the present speed of petrol engines; but at present it is rather the other way, and, as has already been stated, in order to get the best result, the spark has to be timed to occur a shade-before maximum compression. If the ignition arrangements were better, the charge might be ignited exactly at full compression, or, at any rate, not so much before full compression, with a consequent increase in power. There is an undoubted advantage in igniting at different points, for then the combustion has a smaller distance to travel from each igniting point, and the early stages of combustion are accelerated, allowing the timing of the spark to be made a shade later. Fig. 75 illustrates these remarks.

Double Pole Ignition.

The author, with these thoughts in mind, made a trial some time ago of the " Lodge " system of double-pole ignition on a motor cycle engine, and experienced a marked improvement in the running of the engine so fitted. Starting from cold was materially assisted, and owing, no doubt, to the more perfect and rapid combustion of the charge, it was possible to run with less throttle opening than before, thus economising petrol and assisting to keep the engine cool. The system is a very simple one, consisting of a double-pole

106 THE MOTOR CYCLIST'S HANDBOOK.

FIG. 74.—The "Lodge" System of Double-Pole Ignition.

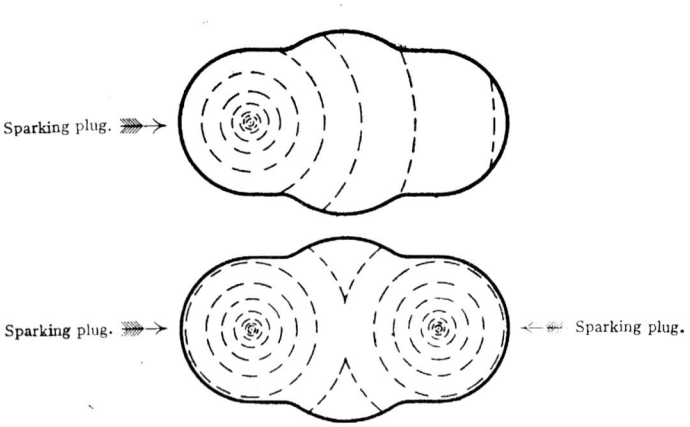

FIG. 75.
EXPANSION OF GASES DIAGRAM.
Upper View: Charge Ignited by a Single Plug. Lower View: Charge Ignited by "Lodge" Double-Pole System.

sparking plug, which is screwed into the cylinder in the ordinary way, and a second plug of standard construction, placed over the exhaust valve or where otherwise convenient. In the engine used the double-pole plug was placed over the inlet valve, and the ordinary plug over the exhaust valve, and the high-tension cable led from the magneto to the double-pole plug. Then a short length of high-tension cable was used to connect up the two plugs, a special fitting being provided on the double-pole plug to allow of this.

A diagram of the arrangement is shown in Fig. 74. With this system in use, the mixture within the cylinder is ignited at two separate points instead of only one, so that more rapid combustion takes place. Increasing the rate of combustion enables the maximum pressure on the piston to be reached earlier in the working stroke without the back-pressure and overheating that would result if the same effect were attempted with one plug, by setting the time of firing so much earlier. Obtaining the maximum pressure early in the stroke gives increase of power, the effect being most noticeable at high speeds.

It may be suggested that much the same result could be arrived at by connecting up two ordinary sparking plugs in parallel, and thus dividing the current from the coil or magneto terminal into two circuits. It becomes a question as to whether a sufficiently intense spark can be obtained at both plugs, and also whether the two will synchronise in the distribution of the current, for, of course, if they fail to do so, the force of the explosion will, as a consequence, suffer, and we may take it that even if a sufficiently intense spark *could* be obtained in these circumstances it would more likely than not be useless, owing to the impossibility of adjusting the gaps of the two plugs to exactly the same distance. The plugs must be in series to obtain synchronism. The mixture must be exploded in the combustion chamber at one precise moment to gain maximum power, and not in successive stages, however finely divided.

Ignition Systems Compared.

In a very few cases motor cycles are fitted with low-tension magnetos, and, where this is done, it is necessary to employ a coil, so that, as in the case of an accumulator, the low-pressure current may be converted into a high-pressure one, this being absolutely essential to the production of a sufficiently intense electric spark. The vast majority of motor cycles are fitted with high-tension magnetos, with double-wound armatures, so that no coil is needed, and there can be no doubt whatever that the latter system is in every way the better one, both on the score of simplicity and efficiency in working.

Each system of ignition has some advantages, and, of course, some disadvantages; but the latter, in the case of the high-tension magneto, are wholly outweighed by the advantages offered.

To sum up the relative claims made on behalf of each system, it may be said that the non-trembler coil requires very little battery current, so the batteries last a long time. It gives a very accurate timing of the ignition, and consumes no power from the engine. Care must be taken that the engine is not stopped in such a position that the current is left on, as, if the switch is closed when the engine is standing in this position, the batteries are sure to be damaged.

The trembler coil affords much the best system for starting and slow running; but, for very high-speed work, the timing of the ignition is not quite as accurate as the other systems. It also consumes more current than a plain or non-trembler coil.

The high-tension magneto is by far the neatest, most compact, and simple to operate of any system. With it no batteries are required, and the wiring is of the most simple character, consisting in fact of only one high-tension insulated wire from the collector terminal on the magneto to the sparking plug. Practically the only disadvantage about a magneto is that it takes a certain proportion of engine power to drive it; but this is small enough to be considered negligible.

Care of the Ignition Appliances.

Longer and more satisfactory service may be obtained from the various appliances employed for ignition if care is taken to maintain the same in clean and proper working condition, and, with a view to assisting the reader in this direction, the author has prepared the following notes, covering the full range of equipment previously described :—

Sparking Plugs.— As before said, there are a large number of different types of sparking plugs, these plugs being

THE IGNITION. 109

FIG. 76.—Sectional View of " Lodge " Sparking Plug.

FIG. 77.—High-tension Cable Wire and Terminal shown Connected and Disconnected.

insulated with eithrr porcelain, steatite, or mica. The plan is sometimes recommended of using very cheap sparking plugs, as a number of these are supposed to be more economical than one good one; but this is a bad plan, as even if it should be more economical (which is doubtful), the plug may fail at a most awkward moment. Much the best plan is to buy plugs of a well-known make, and if the author's long experience stands for anything, the utmost reliance may be placed upon the Bosch, Lodge, and Sphinx ignition plugs. Noteworthy among these is the self-cooling plug of Messrs. Lodge Bros. & Co., which fully justifies the claims made for it.

The Sphinx Manufacturing Co., of Birmingham, supply a range of sparking plugs for motor cycle use, any one of which may be safely relied upon for good and long-continued service. The "Gnat," one of this series, is a specially shallow plug, *i.e.*, one-inch high above cylinder, and thus adaptable to any position that may in special cases be desired. The other plugs are of varying heights, affording different lengths of reach, and all are well made and finished in the best style. The author has used these plugs for a considerable time past, and has found them excellent in every way.

If through faulty lubrication or carburation the plug gets very dirty on the side exposed to the flame, the best way to clean it is to pour petrol into the plug and clean it inside with a small stiff brush. It is of great importance that the plug should be quite gas-tight, and the best way to test for this is by smearing round the joints with oil and then pedalling the engine round, when, if compression is leaking, small bubbles will appear where the oil is smeared on. The plug should be screwed down on to an asbestos washer. With frequent screwing up these copper asbestos washers get hard, and do not make a proper gas-tight seat. They can then be annealed by heating them up to a dull red heat and allowing to cool.

The best distance apart of the sparking points is 0·5 mm. Closer than this would be better for starting; but with a powerful magneto at high speeds, if the points are set any closer there is danger of them fusing together.

A sparking plug should be chosen with a length of reach into the cylinder such that the spark occurs about flush with the inside surface. If the plug projects too far into the cylinder it is liable to get very hot; and if the spark

Fig. 78.
"Bosch"
Sparking
Plug.

Fig. 79.—"Lodge"
Self cooling Sparking
Plug with Ribbed
Exterior.

Fig. 80.—A Range of "Sphinx" Sparking Plugs.

occurs at the back of an opening because the plug has too short a reach, misfiring is very liable to occur, and possibly pre-ignition.

Wipe Contact (for use with trembler coils).—It is important that this should be kept clean, and that there should be a good spring press contact. A little vaseline or oil can be used for lubrication. There should be no looseness in any of the parts, and the surface of the wipe must be perfectly true. The contact-pieces should extend for about 40 degs. In many wipe contacts the " earth " return is through a shaft. This is liable to produce bad contact, and a proper " earthing " terminal is a distinct improvement.

Contact-Makers (for use with trembler coils).—Much the best design is that in which the contact is closed positively, and separated by means of a spring. The contact points are usually of platinum iridium, and if the current can be reversed in direction regularly through these contacts, it will prevent them pitting. All the parts should be kept thoroughly clean, and only the cam actuating the contact points will require a little lubrication.

Contact-Breakers (for use with non-trembler coils).—It is essential that the contact points be made of platinum, or, better, platinum iridium. The points should be separated positively, and be pressed together by means of a spring. Reversing the direction of the current through the points will prevent pitting. A condenser connected across the points is essential, but this is usually contained in the coil.

Cables and Connections.—Both high and low tension cables are best, rubber-covered ; and as nothing lends itself more easily to adulteration than rubber, it is advisable to buy cable from well-known makers only. The total diameter of copper strands should not be too small, both for mechanical as well as electrical reasons. It is most important that all contacts should be thoroughly clean and tight, and the cable should be so supported that there is no chance of the rubber being frayed against a metal edge by the vibration.

Dry Batteries.—These should be chosen with as large capacity as can be conveniently be carried, not only for the reason that they will last longer, but chiefly because the internal resistance, which is an important item with dry batteries, is much less in the case of a dry cell of large capacity. The voltage of a dry cell is usually given as 1·5 ; but

THE IGNITION.

this is measured on open circuit, and when a good current is taken from the cell the pressure drops quickly. It requires four dry cells in series to properly take the place of a 4-volt accumulator.

Accumulators.—The proper charging of accumulators is an important matter. When a 4-volt accumulator shows only 3·6 volts on a voltmeter, it should be recharged at once. When fully charged the accumulator should certainly show 4·4 volts, and immediately after charging, or when being actually charged, it will show a higher pressure than this. With a new accumulator which has never been charged, very great care must be taken to follow out the instructions which are usually supplied with any well-known make. The acid must be of correct quality and density, and the battery must be charged electrically for a long time without stoppage, until both compartments are gassing freely.

The most convenient form of accumulators to use are those mounted in celluloid boxes so that the plates can be seen. Some accumulators have the electrolyte in a jelly form. These do not give as good results as those having ordinary liquid electrolyte. When the accumulator is fully charged, the positive plates are chocolate in colour, and the negative plates grey. When discharged there is very little difference in appearance between the plates.

No acid should be allowed on the outside of the case, and the terminals should be kept very carefully clean. The terminals should be of such a design (usually made with rubber washers on) that the acid cannot creep on to the terminal. Where creeping does occur, thoroughly cleaning up the terminals and smearing all over with vaseline helps to prevent it. It is very important to always keep the level of the liquid above the tops of the plates. Much the best way to keep accumulators for any length of time is to have them in use; but, where this is not possible, a short charge should be given every fortnight, but, in any case, the battery should not be left for more than two months without charging and should be fully charged before being left to stand idle. The author has found the " P.L.," accumulators, manufactured by Messrs. Paish, Lane & Co., of High Holborn, London, W.C., give excellent service. The plates are very substantially made and fitted, and the complete accumulator is a really first-class article sold at a moderate price.

Non-Trembler Coils.—These are very simple instruments, and practically the only important point is to see that they are properly fixed on the machine, all the terminals being clean and screwed up tight. A non-trembler coil should have a larger number of turns and thinner wire in the primary winding than a trembler coil. If this is not so, they are liable to take too large a current. The current taken may be reduced by inserting a resistance; but this is a very inefficient plan, as it is far better to put the resistance into the circuit by means of more turns in the primary winding. When using non-trembler coils, it is very important always to switch off when stopping the engine, as if the contact-breaking points happen to stop in the closed position a heavy current will go through the coil, both damaging it and the accumulators.

Trembler Coils.—The correct adjustment of the trembler makes a considerable difference to the running. The best way of adjusting coils is with special instruments for the purpose; but this method of testing is hardly possible for the average motor cycle rider, and the next best plan is to adjust the trembler while the engine is running. It is impossible to give any definite instructions with reference to the setting of the tremblers, as there are so many different kinds; but by carefully trying different adjustments, the best position will fairly easily be found. As a rule, an extremely light setting gives the best results at very high speeds, but will not give such good starting; and so, as is usually the case, a compromise has to be effected. A good make of trembler coil takes about $\frac{1}{4}$ amp. for a single-cylinder engine, and about $\frac{1}{2}$ amp. for a twin-cylinder engine. If misfiring occurs, see that all the trembler parts are making a thoroughly clean contact, and are perfectly tight. It sometimes occurs that the platinum points come loose in their setting, and this is a difficult fault to detect. The platinum points should exactly coincide, and the surface of contact should be quite level. In trimming the contacts, only a dead smooth file should be used, and as little platinum as possible removed. Reversing the direction of the current through the platinum points prevents pitting, and is economical in platinum.

All coils want mounting in the machine in a place where they will be kept properly clean and free from moisture,

THE IGNITION.

and especially from any possibility of acid spray, or fumes from the accumulator. The coil should be firmly held so that it cannot jolt about.

Adjustments for a Twin-cylinder Engine.—These adjustments are best done with the engine running and, if possible, under load. When a double trembler coil is used, the tremblers should be set as near as possible to precisely the same position. A rough, though not definite, proof is when the two tremblers give the same note. On an engine in which the explosions occur at irregular intervals, the second firing cylinder requires to fire a shade earlier than would be the case if the explosions were exactly at equal intervals.

CHAPTER VIII.

The Transmission; Belt and Chain Drives, Free Engine Clutches, and Variable Speed Gears.

In the preceding chapters we have seen how the motor is constructed, and have followed in succession the principle upon which it works, the production of the fuel it consumes, and the means and apparatus used in the process of ignition. In other words, we have completed the study of our subject

Fig. 81.—Testing the Angle of the Pulley Faces by means of a Gauge Plate.

so far as the *production* of power is concerned, and may now turn our attention to the manner in which that power is applied to its purpose of driving the motor cycle.

Belts and Belt Fasteners.

The most common form of transmission on a motor cycle is that of a "V" belt, working in a similarly shaped pulley on the engine shaft and in a belt rim attached to the rear wheel of the bicycle. This simple method of driving permits of a comparatively narrow belt being employed, as a sufficient

TRANSMISSION AND GEARING. 117

FIG. 81A.—The Dunlop Rubber and Canvas Motor Cycle Belting.

FIG. 82.—"Shamrock-Gloria" Rubber Belt.

FIG. 83.—The "Service" All-Leather Belt.

grip can be obtained in the pulleys by its wedging action; whereas if a flat belt were employed, as in workshop practice, a much wider one would be needed, and the likelihood of slipping would be greatly increased. The angle of the pulley flanges and that of the belt sides must, if a sufficient grip and full power output is to be secured, strictly coincide with one another at 28 degs., and the pulley groove must be sufficiently deep to preclude all possibility of the belt coming into contact with the bottom, for, if that occurs, there will be a considerable, and possibly a total, loss of power, due to slipping. The pulley should be examined when it has been in use some time, to ascertain whether the flanges have worn to an incorrect angle. For testing this a gauge cut to the same width at the top as the belt, and having its sides a true 28 deg. angle, should be used in the manner illustrated in Fig. 81. Round, twisted belts have been used with success on light machines fitted with engines of $1\frac{1}{4}$ or $1\frac{1}{2}$ h.-p. in conjunction with jockey pulleys as tensioning devices. There is, however, a decided tendency to fit even these low-powered models with V belts in the latest practice.

Motor cycle belts are made in several forms—some being of rubber with a tough core of compressed canvas; while others are made of leather strips or layers, riveted or otherwise connected together. Each kind has its advantages, the rubber belt being the cheaper and cleaner of the two, and easier perhaps to adjust; but the leather belt lasts longer and grips better in wet weather. It is customary nowadays to mould rubber belts with transverse grooves on the underside to allow of their bending the more readily round the engine pulley; while, in the case of one well-known make, small grooves are formed at the top also. The great idea is to make the belt as flexible as possible, and the purchaser of a belt should take it in both hands and see whether it will readily conform to a small radius such as it will have to adapt itself to on the engine pulley.

The author has met with very satisfactory experiences with the " Dunlop " and " Shamrock-Gloria " rubber belts; while of the leather ones he has used, the " Watawata " and " Service " belting have given by far the best results. The " Watawata " (Fig. 84) is an extremely flexible belt and its strength is enormous, while the " Service " (Fig. 83)—a slightly cheaper production—runs it very closely on general

FIG. 84.—The "Watawata" Leather Motor Cycle Belt and Fastener.

FIG. 85.—The "Whittle" Motor Cycle Belt; Steel Links with Leather Covering; no fastener required.

merit. All belts stretch when first used, and it may be necessary to shorten them once or twice during the first hundred miles or so run to prevent slipping. A sharp knife (or small saw) and a bradawl or belt punch should be carried at all times, and by the aid of these appliances the task is one of but a few minutes. In the case of leather belts, it is usual to provide several eyelet holes or hollow rivets instead of solid ones for some distance from each end, so that when the necessity for shortening arises the rider is not confronted with the task of drilling out the hole for the fastener screw. It is unwise to go out for a long ride with a leather belt in which none of these openings are provided, for, despite what may be said to the contrary, it is usually a rare job to get rid of the obstructing rivet when out on the road and shortening has to be effected.

As to belt fasteners—their name is legion. The most useful ones are those which permit of the belt being removed from the machine without having to displace the fastener itself. These are called *detachable* fasteners and are made in two separate portions, engaging the one with the other by means of a hook or link, which only needs disconnecting to allow of the belt being immediately and entirely removed. The connecting hooks or links are made in two or three different lengths, so that shortening of the belt may be accomplished without having to cut it; but, of course, when any really appreciable stretch has taken place, the last-named expedient must be resorted to. In the case of the "Whittle" belt (Fig. 85), which is virtually a steel chain encased in leather, no fasteners are required shortening being effected by removing a complete section at a time. The leather pads are held in place by means of ordinary wood screws. This is the belt *par excellence* for the heaviest motor cycle work, and the fact of there being no fastener is a point greatly in its favour.

It is very important that belts for motor cycles shall be suitably proportioned for the work they have to do—say, $1\frac{1}{8}$ ins. wide at top for anything above a 5 h.-p. engine, 1 in. for engines between $3\frac{1}{2}$ h.-p. and 5 h.-p., and either $\frac{3}{4}$-in. or $\frac{7}{8}$-in. for all but the smallest engines (such as $1\frac{1}{2}$ h.-p.), which work very well with $\frac{5}{8}$-in. belts. It is also very important that the belt be maintained in good and flexible condition, rubber ones being sponged over with water or petrol,

FIG. 86.—The "Forward" Belt Fastener: Adjustable and Detachable.

FIG.—87.—The "Terry" Detachable Belt Fastener, with Key for Operating Locking Device.

FIG. 88.—The "Stanley" Detachable Belt Fastener, with Adjusting Links.

FIG. 89.—The "Simplex" Detachable Belt Fastener.

and leather ones scraped and dressed with collan oil occasionally. The belt should be slipped off the pulley when not in use; it should never be run any tighter than is necessary to guard against slipping, for a very tight belt absorbs power and may break. The pulleys should be kept as free as possible from accumulation of grit and grease, and in attaching the fastener care should be taken to place the screw as far back in the belt as circumstances will permit, and perfectly central. Above all, great care should be taken to ensure the belt being in true alignment—*i.e.*, both pulley and belt rim exactly in line with one another. Errors in this direction cause excessive wear of the belt, and, in aggravated cases, may bring about its constant shedding from the pulleys.

FIG. 90.—Chain Transmission of " Scott " Two-stroke Motor Bicycle.

Chain Drive.

Chain-driven motor bicycles are less numerous by far than belt-driven ones. Still, some of the very best makers employ this method exclusively, and there are indications that it will become even more generally adopted in the future. Chain drive was considered to be *the* method of transmission for motor cycles in years gone by, and only because of the great improvements made in belt manufacture was it ever superseded. It is customary to employ two chains—one engaging with the sprocket on the engine shaft, and also with a countershaft at the bottom bracket ; and the other extending rearward from the countershaft to the driving wheel of the bicycle ; this plan doing away with the need for a long chain with its attendant disadvantages of backlash and consequent likelihood of jumping the sprockets. Users of the belt method assert that chain-driven machines are more severe on tyres, less flexible to drive, and more prone to side slip ; while the chains are even more messy to handle in muddy weather and more difficult to repair than belts, while they require greater care all round ; but, on the other hand, the advocates of the chain strenuously deny these allegations, and regard (or affect to regard) the belt users as somewhat behind the times and as poor misguided folk.

FIG. 91.—The Chain Drive of the " Indian " Motor Cycle.

Shaft Drives.

A few makes of motor bicycle, notably the " F.N.," are driven by means of bevel-gear ; the engine shaft in this case running longitudinally instead of transversely to the frame and engaging with a cardan or propeller shaft, carrying at its rearward extremity a small bevel wheel which engages with a larger bevel wheel attached to the rear wheel of the bicycle. This plan is applied to both the four-cylinder and two-speed single-cylinder " F.N." motor bicycles, and has always given satisfaction. Being entirely enclosed, this type of transmission is practically weather-proof and, moreover, is always working under the best conditions to resist wear, all frictional parts being covered with grease.

The "T.A.C." four-cylinder motor bicycles have a similar arrangement, but a worm drive is employed instead of the bevel gear-wheels. This last-named machine, of which an illustration is given on pages 223-4, approximates in many directions to car practice in matters of control, and presents many features which strongly differ from those of any other type of motor cycles.

FIG. 92.—Worm-drive Transmission of the "T.A.C." Four-cylinder Motor Cycles.

Adjustable Pulleys.

We may next proceed to a consideration of transmission developments permitting of varying the gear, the simplest and least expensive of all being the adjustable pulley. This is merely an ordinary V pulley fixed as usual on the engine shaft, but so devised that the outer flange may slide or rotate in such a manner relatively to the inner or fixed flange that the V groove may be widened and the belt caused to sink further into it.

It will readily be seen that when this occurs the relation between the diameter of the engine pulley and that of the belt rim on the back wheel of the bicycle will vary; or to put it more technically, the gear ratio will be lowered. If the pulley has an outside diameter of 5 ins., and the belt rim a diameter of 20 ins., the proportions are as 4 to 1, and the machine is said to have a *gear* of 4 to 1 (the engine pulley making four revolutions to each single revolution of the driving wheel); but, when by manipulating his adjustable pulley the rider lets his belt sink down into the groove so as to pass round, say, a 4-in. instead of a 5-in. radius, as before, he alters this proportion and obtains a gear of 5 to 1, while if he further opens out the flanges he can get a lower gear still. Of course, it is only possible to vary the gear within somewhat narrow limits by this means, for, as has already been pointed out, under no circumstances must the belt be allowed to ride on the bottom of the pulley, while to make the latter much larger in diameter in order to gain a greater range of variation would only be to defeat the object aimed at, and render the higher gears impossible of use except perhaps under the most favourable conditions of running on the flat. Adjustable pulleys make it necessary to employ some means of altering the length of belt to

FIG. 93.—The V.S. Adjustable Pulley.
(A)—Fixed Flange. (B)—Movable Flange. (A1)—Left-hand Thread. (C)—Locking Cap.

suit the varying conditions of gear, and this is where the detachable link fasteners come in very useful indeed. Another method is to cut the belt to the right length for a low gear and to make up the difference required for higher gears by inserting a short length of belt (a few inches only) with an additional fastener, and if the belt is adjusted rather on the tight side it will still grip when the gear is slightly lowered. The adjustable pulley arrangement is a very convenient one, as the gear can be lowered for hill-climbing and raised for level road work without—excepting only in the slightest degree—adding to the complication of the construction.

A simple example of adjustable pulley design is shown in Fig. 93. This type of pulley is fitted to the " V.S." motor cycles and has proved very efficient. The pulley flange (A) is formed in one piece with the boss portion (A^1), which is secured to the taper portion of the engine shaft by means of a feather and outside nut. The boss (A^1) is provided with a left-handed screwed part, and outside that is a right-handed screwed part, as seen. The outer flange (B) of the pulley rotates on the left-handed screwed portion so as to be capable of being moved either nearer or further away from the fixed flange, while the smaller screwed portion of the boss carries a loose cap (C), which serves to lock the movable flange in any desired position. The pressure of the belt (D) against the inside of the loose flange (B) while working, forces the flange outwards against the locking cap (C), so that there is no chance under any circumstances of the flange slipping and automatically lowering the gear by allowing the belt to sink lower into the groove. This pulley gives a range of gears from about $3\frac{3}{4}$-1 to $5\frac{1}{2}$-1.

Numerous other methods of arriving at the same result exist, but space prohibits their being illustrated or described in these pages.

" Wanderer " motor bicycles are fitted with a special arrangement, incorporating an under-geared engine pulley with a device for varying the belt tension from the saddle. Fig. 94 shows the general plan of the arrangement. The pulley is larger than usual and affords a better grip for the belt than where a small pulley has to be encircled. The belt rim on the rear wheel approximates in size to the engine pulley, instead of being from four to five times as large, and this is explained by the fact that the engine shaft carries a small toothed pinion (E), which meshes with the internally toothed surface of the pulley itself. (C) is a fixed shaft supporting the pulley and working on radius (G). The rod (H), which at its top carries a handle arranged for rotary movement, has, at its base, a quick thread engaging with the segmental rack (I). The pulley is capable of being moved eccentrically in relation to the engine shaft by means of this

FIG. 94.—The Undergeared Pulley fitted to " Wanderer " Motor Cycles

rod, and in this manner the belt can be tightened or slackened at will whilst riding. The ratio between the pinion and internal toothed rack is as 3 to 1, while the driving ratio is as $5\frac{1}{2}$ to 1.

Free Engine Clutches.

The next development connected with the transmission is the free engine clutch—a device for allowing the engine to continue in motion, though the bicycle, as a whole, remains

Fig. 95.—The "Mabon" Free Engine Clutch for Motor Cycles.

Fig. 96.—Sectional Elevation of "Mabon" Multiple Disc Clutch and Free Engine Device.

stationary with both its wheels on the ground. A clutch of this description may either be attached to the engine shaft or contained in the hub of the back wheel, and in either case an adjustable pulley may be used as well. A free engine clutch is an undoubted boon to the motor cyclist, for, if nothing else, it does away altogether with any necessity to run alongside the machine to mount, while in traffic, round corners, and on hills, the control of the engine is vastly facilitated. The author has had long experience of the Mabon clutch, and believes it to be the most efficient of any among those designed for attachment to the engine shaft.

The "Mabon" Clutch.

This device, of which a sectional elevation drawing appears on the previous page, combines a free engine adjustable pulley and metal-to-metal disc plate clutch, comprising a drum or box (A) which carries a series of discs or plates and is formed in one piece with the body of the pulley. The outer flange of the pulley is capable of being rotated on the screwed portion of the body to allow of the gear being raised or lowered, on the principle already described.

An inner body portion (E) carrying a second series of plates is secured to the engine shaft in the manner usual with an ordinary pulley, and it will be noticed that the plates carried by the drum (A) and those of the portion (E) just referred to, are arranged so as to interleave or follow one another, in alternate order.

A sleeve (blackened in Fig. 96) is caused to slide in and out of the drum (A) for a limited distance under the action of a strong coil spring (B), the movements of which latter are controlled by means of a forked lever (Fig. 95) pivoted on the end of a short transverse arm connected to a bracket which is bolted to the crank-case as shown. To the outer end of this lever there is attached a Bowden wire, which leads through the bracket (where an adjusting stop is provided) upwards to the handle-bar and there connects with a hand-lever controlled by the rider, this lever being provided with a spring stop so as to avoid the necessity of retaining a hold upon it when the clutch is out. It will thus be seen that the lever on the handle-bar actuates the Bowden wire, the wire moves the outward outer end of the lever backwards and forwards transversely, and this causes its forked end, influenced by the coil spring (B), to work the sleeve in or out of the drum as desired, thus in the first case bringing the two series of plates into frictional contact with one another, when the engine, of course, drives the machine forward in the usual manner, or releasing the plates from contact when the engine runs free without propelling the machine. Between the friction or driving position, and the loose or free engine position—that is to say, when the spring and sleeve are only partly withdrawn—it is possible to obtain almost any degree

FIG. 97.—The Latest Development of the " Mabon " Clutch, showing Handle bar Controlling Mechanism.

of slip required so that the engine, without being altogether released from its load, can be accelerated and its power thereby increased before again letting in the clutch and taking up the drive. In the latest design the forked lever is dispensed with in favour of the rotating sleeve arrangement shown in Fig. 97. This latest device does away with all suggestion of end-thrust, and is particularly sweet in its action.

Motor bicycles fitted with this device can be started from a standstill in the same manner as a car. The rider starts

Fig. 98.—Details of the Lloyd "Auto-Varia" Speed Pulley and Free Engine Device.

his engine by means of the pedals or otherwise, while the rear wheel is jacked up clear of the ground. He then pulls the lever on the handle-bar into the position necessary to free the engine, lets the wheel down on to the ground, and sits astride the saddle, the machine being, of course, entirely motionless the while. Then by gradually engaging the clutch the drive is taken up by the engine and the machine moves slowly forward, gathering speed according to the whim of the rider and his manipulation of the clutch. The clutch-operating lever should always be gradually manipulated, for, if suddenly engaged, the engine will be unable to accommodate itself to the load and will come to a stop. If traffic of sufficient density to impede his progress confronts him, the rider, by disengaging the clutch, can bring the machine to a standstill, keeping the engine running, and re-engaging when an opportunity for going ahead presents itself. If obstructed on a hill and the speed of the engine falls below what is necessary to maintain the power required, it can be restored by allowing the engine to run partially or wholly free for a few seconds, and in a hundred different circumstances the clutch will be found useful in controlling the motor cycle. It is, perhaps, superfluous to add that while sitting astride the stationary machine the rider maintains his balance by placing one foot on the ground.

The Lloyd " Auto-Varia " Pulley.

The " Auto-Varia " speed pulley and free engine arrangement of the Lloyd Motor and Engineering Company is an ingenious device in which the ratio of the gear adjusts itself automatically to the gradient of a hill. The adjustable flange of the pulley is forced outwards by the wedging action of the belt against the tension of a series of springs placed radially on the outside, as shown in the drawing (Fig. 99). As the load on the engine increases with the grade, and more power is exerted, the pulley is caused, by the added belt pressure, to automatically expand, compressing the springs and allowing the belt to sink deeper into the groove and provide a lower gear. Similarly, as the load decreases and the engine puts forth less power, the belt pressure against the flange lessens, and the springs, reacting, close the pulley in, and the belt is caused to rise and assume a higher gear.

Free engine is obtained by forcing a roller in between the

TRANSMISSION AND GEARING. 133

FIG. 99.—The "Auto-Varia" Speed Pulley.

FIG. 99A.—"L.M.C." Motor Bicycle, fitted with Lloyd Auto-Varia Speed Pulley and Free Engine.

pulley flanges, and expanding them until the belt drops on to a ball-bearing ring at the bottom. This roller is carried as seen, at the lower extremity of a side lever, conveniently arranged and held in position by the bracket gate attached to the top tube of the frame where it can be manipulated easily from the saddle. When the lever is in the front notch, the roller is out of engagement. The intermediate notch gives a low gear for starting, and the rearmost notch free engine. It is claimed that the belt cannot slip when in the low gear, because the coil springs are always exerting an even pressure on the loose flange.

Hub Clutches.

Other free engine devices are those which are fitted in the hub of the rear wheel of the bicycle, and their manipulation is effected by means of levers placed within easy and convenient reach of the rider's foot. This system has the advantage of allowing the engine to be started without the necessity of jacking up the rear wheel clear of the ground, so that the rider may take his seat, press down one of the pedals sharply, and the engine will start, all being then in immediate readiness to go ahead by simply engaging the clutch. To permit of this, the belt rim is arranged to revolve independently of the wheel during such times as the clutch is "out," and the act of engaging the latter causes the rim and wheel to become locked and to revolve together.

The " Rex " Free Engine Clutch.

A good example of this type of clutch is shown in Fig. 100, which illustrates the "Rex" multiple plate clutch fitted to the "tourist" pattern motor bicycles of that name. The two main sections are the outer shell, to which is attached the wheel, and the inner sleeve, to which is coupled the belt pulley wheel. On the wheel section are eight feather keys, and these eight keys register with eight slots on the metal compensating external cone. The pulley section is also fitted with eight feather keys, on which slide two internal cones. These internal cones are pressed home concentrically by means of springs, thereby giving a rigid drive. A free engine is obtained on the coarse screw (F). This operation causes the plunger (G) to compress the springs (J), which act on clutch

TRANSMISSION AND GEARING. 135

FIG. 100.—The "Rex" Free Engine Clutch, fitted in Hub of Rear Wheel.

FIG. 101.
The "Triumph"
Free Engine
Device.

cones. It is operated by foot-pedals, similar to the " Rex " light clutch and two-speed gear.

It will be noticed that the hub contains two ball races—namely, (N) the free engine ball race, and (P) the driving ball race. This is a great feature of the Rex plate hub, and renders it exceptionally free in its action, and, by obviating friction, prevents undue wear and strain in the working parts of the hub. The engine is started when the machine is stationary by a downward thrust of the pedal.

The "Triumph" Clutch.

Another good example of the hub type of clutch is that of the Triumph Company, illustrations of which are appended. This clutch consists of a number of grooved steel plates, half of which engage on the axle and the other half in the ribs of the hub shell, these plates being held in compression by four springs. The drive is absolutely solid and there is claimed to be no end thrust. When the clutch is out of action, the back wheel runs on a pair of ball-bearings, as in an ordinary hub. The clutch is operated by means of a rod, to which is attached a combined toe-and-heel pedal fitted to the footrest on the right side of the machine ; and in order to start the engine the rider (while seated in the saddle) puts the clutch out of action by pressing down the toe pedal, and next gives the crank pedal a smart push downwards. The clutch is then engaged by pressing down the heel pedal and allowing the toe pedal to gradually engage. The makers recommend the use of water-cooled oil for lubricating the clutch, and the hub should be periodically flushed with paraffin and well oiled afterwards. The weight added to the machine by fitting the clutch is about 10 lbs.

In other cases the engine is started by means of a handle engaging with an extension on the axle of the rear wheel, and in this case also the belt rim revolves apart from the wheel itself. This system is known as the " live " axle system, and is incorporated with some of the most successful two-speed gears adapted to motor cycles.

It is a very difficult, if not an impossible, task to start the engine by means of a handle secured to the engine shaft, where magneto ignition is employed, owing to the fact that a sufficient speed of rotation cannot conveniently be got on the armature of the magneto by this means to produce a spark of suitable intensity to fire the mixture; but if the handle is affixed to a countershaft, or, as before described, to the live axle of the rear wheel, the extra leverage so obtained makes it an easy matter to set the parts revolving at a good speed before dropping the exhaust lever and setting the engine going.

FIG. 101A.—Hub Free Engine Clutch, "Triumph" Motor Cycles.
Showing Control Mechanism.

Incidentally, a free engine clutch materially assists the rider when wheeling his machine along, as he must sometimes do. He can then disengage the clutch, and by so doing stop the motion of the engine, so that there is no need to hold the exhaust lifter up to release compression, and both hands are left entirely free for handling the machine.

Variable Speed Gears.

We may next briefly consider the subject of variable speed gears for motor cycles. These are made in several forms, the majority affording a single change of gear, with a neutral or free engine position as well. These are known as two-speed gears in that they provide a high gear for fast running, under normal conditions, and a low gear for hill-climbing and for use in circumstances (such as when driving in thick traffic, and so on) which make it inconvenient to

FIG. 102.—Starting a New Hudson Motor Bicycle by the Free Engine Method. Engine running, but machine stationary. Rider steadies himself and machine until ready to engage the clutch.

employ a high gear. Appliances of this kind are not confined to any particular class of machine, nor are they restricted for use with any one type of transmission alone. They are used alike with belt, chain, and shaft drives, and are fitted by some makers as a standard feature, while almost

TRANSMISSION AND GEARING. 139

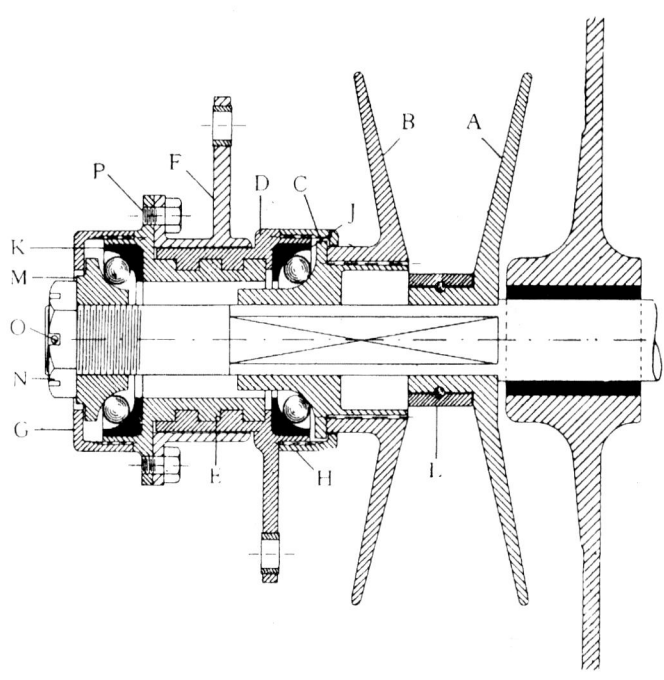

FIG. 103.—Section through "Gradua" Variable Speed Gear (Expanding Pulley Type).

(A)—Fixed Inner Flange
(B)—Sliding Flange.
(C)—Sliding Cone screwed in Flange B.
(D)—Female Screw.
(E)—Male Screw.
(F)—Lever for top Gear Rod.
(G)—Outer Retaining Cap.
(H)—Inner Retaining Cap.
(J)—Ball Race in D.
(K)—Ball Race in E.
(L)—Ball Bearing Ring on Flange A.
(M)—Left-hand Cone on Shaft.
(N)—Left-hand Lock Nut.
(O)—Split Pin.
(P)—Set Screws.

any motor bicycle can be equipped with some form of variable gear, and the plan is coming into greater favour every year.

Where the *frequent* carrying of an extra passenger under genuine touring conditions is contemplated, a variable gear becomes practically a necessity, although quite a large measure of satisfaction can be obtained under these circumstances even with a single-geared machine. The author, however, strongly recommends prospective " passenger " motor cyclists to invest in a variable geared machine or have their existing mount fitted with a device of this kind, failing which they should at least employ an adjustable pulley and free engine clutch combined.

The Chater-Lea and T.A.C. (Wilkinson Sword Company) firms go so far as to provide three-speed gears on their motor cycles, and more recently the Armstrong Triplex Company has introduced a three-speed gear and free engine device adaptable to light or medium weight motor cycles fitted with engines up to about 3 h.-p.

The " Infinitely Variable " (or Expanding Pulley) Type.

Apart from these gears, there is another type known as the " infinitely variable " gear, by means of which the ratio may be altered between the limits of the highest and lowest gears by small and indefinite degrees, instead of, as is the case with a two-speed gear, only allowing of the one change—*i.e.*, from high to low. Thus, if the topmost gear is, say, 4 to 1, and the lowest 8 to 1, *any* intermediate ratio between these two points can be obtained by manipulation of the operating mechanism. The "Gradua" gear (Figs. 103 and 104) is an excellent example of this type, and the changes in the ratio are obtained by allowing the pulley to expand or contract and the belt to rise or fall in the groove, while the back wheel of the bicycle is caused to move either backward or forward in the frame stays to maintain an even belt tension. The gear is manipulated by means of a rotatable handle above the top tube of the frame, and the turning of this handle (which actuates bevel and chain-wheel mechanism of a very simple kind) effects the movements of the pulley and rear wheel above referred to. It will be readily understood that when the belt is at the *top* of the pulley the bicycle wheel is at the end of its forward travel and the gear is the highest obtainable, and when the belt has been allowed (by operating the controlling mechanism) to sink down into the pulley as far as possible without coming in contact with the bottom, the wheel is practically at the end of its rearward travel, and the gear is the lowest obtainable; while any intermediate variation provides at once a *slightly* higher or lower gear as may be desired. The arrangement permits of the utmost flexibility being obtained from the engine and almost any condition of running can be immediately provided for, however quickly changing it may be; whereas with a two-speed gear it must be either the high or the low gear, and sometimes the latter has to be kept in use longer than is advantageous, because to jump up from, say, 8 to 1 to 4 to 1 would, under certain conditions, cause the engine to labour, if not to stop altogether.

FIG. 104.—" Zenith " Motor Bicycle fitted with " Gradua " Expanding Pulley Gear Mechanism.

Free engine is obtained in the infinitely variable type of gear by allowing the pulley flanges to expand to such an extent that the belt comes in contact with the bottom where a ball-bearing slip ring is provided for it to ride upon, which it does without, of course, communicating the drive to the rear wheel of the bicycle, as it has no grip on the pulley flanges. Directly, however, the operating mechanism is brought into play, and the flanges are slightly contracted, or moved in towards one another, the belt at once grips and the drive is taken up on the lowest gear, and so on up

FIG. 105.—The "Mabon" Expanding Pulley Variable Gear.
(A)—Carrier Plate attached to Crank-case.   (B)—Plate Carrying Pulley.
(*a*)—Drum or Sleeve forming part of Plate B.   (*c*)—Pulley Carrier Spindle.   (*d*)—Sleeve upon which Outer Pulley Flange slides.
(*e*)—Sliding Cam Pieces actuating Pulley Flange.

to the highest gear, if desired, by continued manipulation of the handle.

The " Mabon " (Fig. 105) is another infinitely variable speed gear for motor cycles. The details of this gear were, at the time of writing, undergoing some slight modifications prior to its being definitely placed upon the market. The engine shaft carries a toothed sprocket wheel, which drives, by means of a short Hans-Renold chain, a spindle aft carrying the belt pulley, which latter occupies a position immediately at the rear of the engine shaft and between it and the bottom bracket. The pulley flanges are caused to expand and contract by a simple cam mechanism actuated by the rider from the saddle, and when at the bottom of the groove the belt rides on a ball-bearing slip ring and, as before explained, provides a free engine.

The means adopted for maintaining the belt tension, irrespective of changes in the gear ratio, is an ingenious and very simple one. The spindle carrying the pulley is mounted upon a cast-iron plate or carrier which, at its forward end, is provided with a circular drum or sleeve encircling the engine shaft. This drum portion moves about the engine shaft together with the carrier portion, in either an upward or downward direction, taking the pulley with it as a matter of course. The movement of the parts is a radial one, and as the pulley falls the flanges expand, and the belt, sinking further into the groove, the gear is lowered. Oppositely, as the pulley rises the flanges contract and the gear is raised, while at the same time the distance between the pulley centre and that of the rear wheel increases as the gear is lowered and decreases as it is raised, so that as the effective diameter of the pulley varies the distance between the centres varies in accordance with it.

The author tested this gear for some considerable time on a powerful twin-cylinder motor bicycle and side car, and, experimental as portions of it at that time were, the gear emerged triumphant from the searching and prolonged investigation in the most creditable manner possible. In all some 5,000 miles were covered without any serious defect showing itself.

Two-speed Gears : The " V.S."

Of the two-speed motor cycle gears at present on the market, one of the most successful is that of the V.S.

Company. This gear consists of planet pinions operated in such a manner that when one of each of the two sets of pinion wheels is held back by the brake designed for the purpose, the pair of wheels which carry the hub shell rotate around the pinion wheels. When running upon the high gear the hub shell is connected with the driving wheel of the bicycle by a toothed clutch: at such times—which, of course, greatly

FIG. 105.—The "V.S." Two-speed Gear and Free Engine (mounted in rear Wheel Hub).

predominate—all gears are entirely out of operation. The gear is actuated by means of a lever placed on the left-hand side of the tank with a quadrant to guide it. The central position gives free engine; forward position high gear; and backward position low gear. The method of starting and controlling the gear is very simple. The engine is first of all started by a push-down of the pedal and the lever placed in central (or free engine) position. Then all being in readiness for the actual start (the rider having taken his seat), the control lever is pulled slowly backwards until the brake engaging the pinion gears begins to grip. The machine will then start off slowly, but will pick up speed if the lever is pulled still further rearwards. The top speed is put into operation by slowly pushing the lever into extreme forward position, and it is advisable when doing this to lift the exhaust valve so as to reduce the power of the engine. Immediately,

Fig.—107.—Operating Lever, " V.S." Two-speed Gear.

however, the clutch is engaged the exhaust lever can be dropped, and the machine will then run on top speed in the same way as does the ordinary direct drive motor cycle. The reduction on the low speed is 50 per cent.

The " Roc " Gear.

The " Roc " two-speed gear and free engine clutch with live axle and handle starting has been developed by the makers, Messrs. A. W. Wall, Ltd., Birmingham, to a high pitch of

Fig. 108.—The "Roc" Two-speed Gear and Free Engine, of which extensive use is made for Motor Cycles.

excellence. They not only fit it to the motor bicycles of their own manufacture, but also supply complete "conversion" sets adaptable to almost any standard machine. The gear is constructed on the epicyclic principle—that is to say, with small pinions actuating central driving and driven pinions, with which they engage the gears; in fact, being always in mesh.

Referring to the accompanying drawing (Fig. 108), the live back axle (A) runs in bearings (D) held in the frame. At one end of the axle the fixed cone (F) is attached, and on the other end there is an adjustable cone (E) which gives all adjustments to the hub, thus making the gear and hub ball-bearing throughout. At one end of the hub (G) is attached the hub pinion (J). Behind this pinion is the phosphor-bronze bush (H) on which runs one side of the gear-box (H1). The belt rim centre (W) is built up on the live axle (A) which axle also forms the driving gear (L). The belt rim centre (W) is formed of two pressed steel plates, and riveted to this is a driving plate which meshes into the gear (L) which is fixed to the spindle. Inside the gear-box are three pinions (M) set equidistant from the gear attached to the spindle of the hub, and these pinions run on a hardened and ground steel pin (N), and through the centre of this the gear-box is clamped together by the bolt (O). On the outside of the gear-box are two band brakes—one being attached to the belt rim (W), and the other one (V) is attached to the frame. The method of operating the band brake (U) is as follows: One end of the live axle is bored to receive a taper push-piece (Q), which in turn actuates the rod (Q1) operating the lever (R) connected to the hand brake. When the spindle is rotated by means of the starting handle it carries the belt rim round with it in a forward direction, giving the engine pulley several turns necessary to start the engine. The gear-box then revolves in the opposite direction to the belt rim through the action of the pinions. When pressure is applied to the band brake (V), it holds the gear-box stationary to the driving member; the low gear is then in action. On the other hand, when pressure is applied to the push-piece (Q) it tightens the band brake (U)—which is a fixture to the belt rim—on to the gear-box, thus driving *en bloc*, and the top gear is obtained. It will be noticed that when either the high or the low gear is at work there is practically no friction taking place in the hub.

FIG. 109.—"Roc" Two-speed Gear and Free Engine, with Operating Mechanism. Shown as fitted to a Humber Motor Bicycle.

When starting a motor cycle fitted with this arrangement, it is only necessary to raise the exhaust valve lifter and then rotate the live axle of the back wheel a few revolutions, dropping the exhaust lifter in the ordinary way when the engine is revolving at a fair speed. Then it is an easy matter to engage the low gear and move away slowly in a similar manner to a car, putting in the higher gear at the first opportunity.

The " P. & M." Gear.

Another well-known motor cycle two-speed gear is the Phelon & Moore, fitted as standard on the machines manu-

FIG. 110.—The " P. & M." (Phelon & Moore) Two-speed Gear.

factured by the firm of that name (which machines are usually referred to as the P. & M., for short). This gear is adapted for chain drive, as seen in the drawing. Briefly, the mechanism consists of expanding rings made of bronze which work within hardened steel rings carefully ground to shape. The rings are expanded by wedge bars in combination with rollers suitably placed and operated by a ball disc bearing and fixed through a rod which passes through the main axle, and upon which the whole of the two-speed gear revolves. Cavities are provided in the rings for the storage of grease for lubrication and, once charged, this will last for a long time. As before said, the transmission is by chains, of which there are three—viz., high gear chain from the sprocket on the engine shaft to another sprocket on the countershaft, a similar arrangement for the low gear, and finally a chain drive from the countershaft to the rear wheel of the bicycle. The drawing (Fig. 110) shows the construction of the gear very plainly. The spring bronze rings are expanded by the movement of the wedge bars. When the thickest part of the wedge bars lies between the rings neither ring is expanded, and, therefore, both the gear-wheels run free instead of with the body of the gear. As the small sprocket driving to the back wheel is part of the gear itself, it follows that when neither of the gear-wheels are gripped by the expansion of the rings, the power of the engine is not communicated to the driving wheel. It is also obvious that the movement of the wedge bars in either direction will cause one of the bronze rings to expand and transmit the engine power to the back wheel, the drive being direct on both gears. The solid spindle operates the wedge bars, the thrust being taken by a double ball-bearing. Provision is made for starting the engine by handle on the countershaft, the engine running free until the low gear is engaged. The gear ratio of the " P. & M." motor bicycles are $4\frac{1}{2}$ to 1 (high) and 8 to 1 (low); while for those who desire to use their machines for taking a side car the gears are 5 to 1 and 9 to 1. The drive is taken up very gradually with this type of gear owing to the sliding action of the wedge bars, and, unless the rider is very careless indeed, he cannot very well injure any part of the mechansim.

The P. & M. gear has been applied to certain other makes of motor cycles, and in one case the countershaft is placed forward of the engine and carries a belt pulley, in addition to the sprocket, the final drive to the rear wheel being by belt, thus combining the two systems of transmission.

In the " Indian " two-speed gear and free engine clutch, illustrated on pages 152-3 in section, the gear-box is fitted between the engine and rear wheel and occupies the position of the usual bottom bracket. The whole box can be made to slide on the frame, so that the engine chain can be easily and quickly adjusted. The clutch is a development of the compensating sprocket which has always been

TRANSMISSION AND GEARING.   151

fitted on Indian motor cycles, and acts as a shock absorber to the transmission.

Referring to the illustration, the four pinions (A, B, C, and D) are always in mesh. Gears (B and D) are solid together and bushed to run on a stationary lay shaft, which is firmly keyed into steel bushings pressed into the aluminium gear case (G). The engine drives by chain on to the loose sprocket (O), and when the clutch is in, the drive is communicated to the main shaft (X). the central portion of which is castellated and upon which slides the dog clutch (P_1). This clutch has four heavy teeth on each face, corresponding with similar teeth on the loose pinion (C) and the loose sleeve (Y). Clutch (P_1) is operated by forks on the shaft (P), which latter extends to the outer case and is connected by rods and levers with a change speed handle on the top frame tube.

It is evident that if clutch (P_1) is moved to the left it locks shaft (X) to the loose sleeve (Y), causing a direct drive from the sprocket (O) to the sprocket (Z), which latter is firmly locked to (Y). The final drive is by chain from the sprocket (Z) to the rear wheel.

If, on the other hand, clutch (P_1) is moved to the right to engage the pinion (C), the drive will be from the sprocket (O) on to the main shaft (X), through the clutch (P_1) to the pinions (C and D) on the countershaft, thence by means of pinions (B and A)—which latter is firmly keyed to (Y)—to the sprocket (Z).

The neutral position is found by placing the dog clutch (P_1) midway between the pinion (C) and the sleeve (Y).

It will be noticed that ball-bearings of ample dimensions are used wherever necessary.

The clutch is of the multiple disc type, the frictional surfaces in this case being respectively steel and Raybestos. The engine drives by chain on to the sprocket ring (O), which latter is free to rotate around shaft (X), as it runs on small rollers carried by the back plate (N), (N) being firmly fixed to (X) by the keys (N_1). (O) carries with it the plate ring (O_1) by means of dogs which lock them together. The plates (M M_1 and N) are Raybestos faced and rotate with the main shaft (X), as they are all three held together by pins (not shown in drawing). The plate (M), however, is free to slide endways on the shaft (X), and is normally forced towards (N) by the four springs (S) in the thimbles (T). In this to (M, M$_1$) and (N) by the friction between their surfaces, the position the clutch is in, and the rings (O, O$_1$) are firmly held drive passing to the main shaft (X) and thence into gear-box.

Fig. 111.—The "Indian" Two-speed Gear and Free Engine Clutch. Cross Section (*through Gear-box* on line *a-b*, Fig. 112.)

The releasing of the clutch is accomplished by a pin that slides inside the main shaft and is operated by the coarse pitch screw (F), which in turn is operated by the lever (E); this lever being connected to a foot lever conveniently situated on the left-hand side of the motor cycle. This pin butts against the adjusting screw (E) and separates the plates (M and N), thus freeing the gear ring (O) and allowing the engine to run idle. This arrangement enables the rider to set the clutch for any amount of slip he desires, and it will remain in the position adjusted. The clutch is easily accessible and easily adjusted, and all end thrust is eliminated while in the driving position.

Fig. 112.—The "Indian" Two-speed Gear and Free Engine Clutch, Sectional Elevation. (*Clutch on left, Gear-box on right.*)

Engine-Shaft Two-speed Gears.

In addition to the gears already described, there are others —such, for instance, as the N.S.U., Fit-All, and Osborne— which are carried on the engine shaft, the last-named providing four speeds and a free engine. They are adaptable to almost any make of motor bicycle, but their use naturally adds rather considerably to the weight carried by the shaft—a point of small significance perhaps where the engine is primarily designed for the purpose, but one which must be considered where the engine has been converted to a two-speed one by the addition of a gear fitted on the main shaft.

FIG. 113.—The "Millennium Fit-All" Two-speed Gear; adaptable to the Engine Shaft of the majority of Motor Bicycles.

Fig. 113 shows the "Millennium Fit-All" gear manufactured by Lake & Elliott, Braintree, Essex, and which is, it is claimed, readily adaptable to practically any machine. The primary sun wheel (B) is fitted to the engine shaft (A) in the place of the ordinary belt pulley, and fastened by the sleeve nut (C), which takes the place of the ordinary nut. (K) is the secondary sun wheel which is mounted on the primary sun (B) and runs on adjustable ball-bearings. The belt pulley (I) is fastened to the secondary sun wheel (K)— it is now screwed left-hand instead of being keyed as shown. The gear-box (H) has one bearing on the primary sun wheel, and the other on the pulley (I) and carries three pairs of planet pinions (L)—the larger of the pair gears with the primary sun wheel (B), and the smaller with the secondary. For the low gear the gear case (H) is held stationary by the band brake (G), then the sun wheel (B) drives the secondary sun (K) through the planet pinions (L). The sizes of these gears are arranged to give the required reduction. F is a leather-faced friction clutch, having a square hole in the centre, and is mounted on the squared end of the primary sun wheel (B) and is free to slide thereon. J and J_1 are a pair of inclined plane levers by which the clutch can be forced on to the gear-box (H). This carries the whole gear-box, gears, and belt pulley, round the primary sun wheel (B), and gives the high or normal gear with no extra strain of friction except a negligible amount in the ball-bearings of J and J_1.

Fig. 113A.—The "Millennium Fit-All" Two-speed Gear in position.

The "Armstrong-Triplex N.P." 3-speed gear and clutch, designed for motor-cycles with engines up to 3 h.-p., is shown in Fig. 114.

Is a Variable Speed Gear Necessary?

Variable speed gears naturally add some complication to machines equipped with them, but the parts are usually so

Fig. 114.—The "Armstrong-Triplex" Three-speed Gear (for Motor Cycles of medium horse-power).

(A)—Gear operating mechanism.
(B)—Belt Rim Spokes.
(C)—Internally toothed lower Gear ring.
(D)—Thread on to which Hub Shell is screwed.
(EF)—Planet Wheels.
(G)—Sun Wheel.
(H)—Carrier holding eight Planet Wheels.
(I)—Top-speed Gear Ring.
(J)—Clutch Springs.
(K)—Disc Clutch.
(L)—Clutch operating mechanism.
(M)—Hub Shell.
(N)—Free Wheel Sprocket.
(O)—Square Studs which fit the Driving Discs of the Plate Clutch.

TRANSMISSION AND GEARING. 157

Fig. 115.—Three-speed Gear Box, T.A.C. 4-cylinder Motor Cycles.

Fig. 116.—Change-speed Lever (gate principle) T.A.C. Motor Bicycle.

substantially designed and well-made and assembled that little trouble is experienced with them. The presence of such mechanism on the motor cycle gives the rider a feeling of confidence when travelling over difficult or crowded roads, and conduces to better driving, greater all-round convenience, and much more pleasure than would otherwise be possible. At the same time, where expense is a serious object, or the fear of added mechanism to look after acts as a strong deterrent, the motor cyclist may obtain practically all he wants on average roads, with a single-geared machine—of course, fitted with an adjustable pulley. Gears add weight and cause some appreciable extra wear of the tyres. They are by no means dispensable, unless, as before said, two riders are to be infrequently carried; and the beginner, at all events, will do well to start operations with a single-geared machine of as simple construction as possible. As regards the use and manipulation of multiple gears the reader will find a few simple directions in Chapter XII, which deals in part with Hints on the Driving of the Motor Cycle.

CHAPTER IX.

LUBRICATION.

THE lubrication of a motor cycle engine is a matter requiring the most careful attention at *all* times; for not only does the efficiency of the engine depend very largely indeed upon it, but a distinct element of danger to the working parts arises should any serious neglect occur in this direction.

In the case of a steam engine the pistons, slide-valves, and other rapidly reciprocating parts, work under much more favourable conditions than is possible with an internal combustion engine, for there the steam itself imparts a certain amount of lubrication and moisture, whereas in a petrol engine —in which everything works at a high speed and in a very high temperature—the tendency is to run dry unless the parts are continuously and adequately supplied with a proper means of lubrication. In the superheated locomotives now coming into favour on railways, special lubricants have to be employed for the cylinders and valves because of the dryness of the steam under high superheat; the steam at the highest temperatures partaking almost of the nature of a gas and containing many of the characteristics of petrol and similar vapours.

The means employed for lubricating motor cycle engines is known as the splash system, the oil being pumped into the crank-case, where, by capillary action, the flywheels, in revolving, throw it upwards and in various directions, so that it reaches every bearing and every part requiring to be lubricated. The engine thus, in a sense, looks after itself so long as a sufficient level of oil is maintained in the crank-case for distribution by the flywheels and the motor cyclist must always make it his particular business to see that such a level *is* maintained.

A portion of the tank of the motor bicycle is set apart for carrying a supply of lubricating oil, generally about one quart, but less in the case of lightweight machines with small engines. A hand force pump is provided, by means of which the oil is drawn from the lubricating compartment of the tank and forced into the crank-case through a pipe connecting the pump therewith. The oil compartment and pumps are now-a-days placed, as a rule, near the after end of the tank so that the plunger may be conveniently operated by the rider, instead of, as formerly, being carried near the steering head, when it was necessary to bend forward with outstretched hand to reach the plunger. The precise construction can be gathered from an examination of the folding plate.

Character of the Lubricant.

A great deal depends upon the brand and consistency of the lubricating oil used, and readers are *specially* cautioned against accepting oil from a big drum bearing no name, and having nothing but the wayside vendor's recommendation to back it. The makers of the machine are always ready to suggest to the purchaser which particular brand and grade of lubricating oil is most suitable for the engine ; but this apart, it is quite safe to employ any of the well-known brands which can be purchased in distinctly coloured sealed cans bearing the manufacturer's name and trademark. Air-cooled engines require a much thicker oil than water-cooled ones, the reason being, of course, that the great heat generated within the cylinders is, in the former case, entirely dependent for its dissipation upon the surrounding currents of air, and the greater the heat the more rapidly will the oil be thinned and the limit of its lubricating properties reached. If too thick an oil be used the tendency of the piston to " gum up " in the cylinder when the engine has cooled down after working is increased, and the difficulty of starting again is largely augmented. On the other hand, if the oil be too thin the engine, although given a surplus supply, will not be adequately lubricated, and wherever a chance presents itself the oil will escape from the crank-case and splash all over the outside of the engine. And it should never be forgotten that it is the inside and not the outside of the engine that requires lubricating, so that all jointings must be kept tight and the tappets be a good (though freely working) fit in their guides to prevent oil splashing out through them. After much experimenting with various

brands, the author has settled down to the use of Price's
"Huile-de-Luxe" for the winter, and the same maker's grade
"A" or "B" for summer use.

The Effects of Over (and Under) Lubricating.

If too much oil be given, the carbonised deposits on piston
and cylinder will be excessive, and the engine may at times
be caused to misfire or stop altogether, owing to the sparking
plug points getting fouled. A well-made plug will often
spark quite efficiently in oil; but when over-lubrication is
persistently indulged in, sooner or later (and generally sooner
than later) a particle of burnt matter gets carried along with
the splashings of oil to the plug and lodges between the points
and the central electrode, thus short-circuiting the current by
doing away with the air-gap and stopping the ignition of the
mixture. It is immaterial when this happens, whether
the sparking plug has one point or more, the short-circuiting
being complete if only one of the gaps gets filled in as described.
Twin engines, in which the sparking plugs are placed more or
less horizontally, are specially prone to this trouble.

But the evils arising from *over* lubrication are as nothing
compared with those which *under* lubrication may bring
about. Not so much the constant sparing use of the oil,
but real neglect of the lubrication for long periods at a time.
Presumably, no one possessing the least common-sense would
do such a thing wilfully, yet it remains a fact that splendid
engines have been damaged, and some actually ruined,
by inadequate use of the oil pump. If the engine becomes
denuded of oil altogether, and is made to continue working
at a high speed in that condition for any length of time,
the natural consequence is that either the bearings or the
piston (perhaps both) will seize up and become wholly im-
movable until drastic methods are employed to release them;
and once any part has seized it is generally a matter for
the repairer, while a new cylinder altogether, to say nothing
of other parts affected, may have to be fitted and a considerable expense thereby incurred.

Channels or oil-ways are cut on the insides of the crank
case, and wherever it is necessary the oil should work its
way—that is, between the shafts or pins and the bearings
in which they work—and the splashing of the lubricant is so
thoroughly performed that not only the main portions of

the engine obtain a sufficient supply (when a proper level is maintained in the crank-case), but the timing and magneto gears are lubricated as well.

Automatic Lubrication.

The hand-pump method of lubrication is at best rather a crude one. It leaves a lot to be decided by the "human element," in the form of the driver's individual attention; and with a view in large measure to superseding this, the makers are in some instances fitting sight-feed drip lubricators by means of which the lubrication of the engine is automatically performed, the only matter with which the driver need then concern himself being the primary one of setting the rate of feed, which is effected by means of a small needle valve, adjusted by a handle, as seen in the sketch, Fig. 117, which illustrates a J.A.P. automatic lubricator, the functions of which are as follows:—By means of a non-return valve a partial vacuum is set up in the oil-pipe and a steady and even supply of oil is drawn through a needle valve and glass barrel. The latter enables the rider to see at a glance if the oil is coming through, and in what quantity, and a small tap controlling the needle valve adjusts the supply. The lubricator, once set, is quite automatic, and the faster the engine runs the more oil is admitted, or the reverse. At the first outset, with a new machine, it is advisable to open the needle valve one-and-a-half turns. This will give plenty of lubrication and it can afterwards be economised to the drivers' own ideas.

FIG. 117.—"J.A.P." Automatic Sight-Feed Lubricator.

In warm weather the drip system may be relied upon entirely, and it has the great advantage of maintaining a constant flow of oil to the engine, instead of there being, as already pointed out, a surplus part of the time and a shortage at other times. The rate of feed can be automatically increased when extra work is called for, and decreased when the conditions are normal or less arduous; and only in very cold weather is there likely to be any difficulty in getting the device to work properly. This automatic system is usually supplemented by an ordinary hand pump, so that should any derangement arise, the older method can be fallen back upon, and in some cases the two systems are actually combined in one fitting.

Symptoms of Oil Shortage.

The motor cyclist should make it a practice, whilst riding, to keep his ears open for any unusual sounds arising from the engine, and if in any doubt whatever the best plan is to inject a charge of oil. Should a decided acceleration follow, it may be taken as certain that the engine was calling for more oil, and the unaccustomed sound will probably disappear almost at once. Preliminary signs of overheating are a decided slowing down and labouring of the engine, coupled with a more or less metallic noise, and should these symptoms develop, the remedy must be quickly applied, for otherwise the next thing to happen may be a partial or total seizure. In these circumstances—*i.e.*, when the indications are pronounced—it is well to stop and allow the engine to cool down and charges of oil should be worked into the bearings by pedalling before starting the engine up again.

The author once came up with a motor cyclist who complained, as he rode along, that his engine seemed to be falling off in speed. Asked how long it was since the last charge of oil had been injected, he said he had quite forgotten. On two successive charges being given, the engine at once accelerated in a most remarkable manner, and tackled a steep hill immediately afterwards in splendid style. These spurts, after lubricating, *always* indicate oil shortage, and it is the rider's business to make sure that the same thing does not recur.

General Hints on Lubrication.

Attention should occasionally be given to the force pump, the plunger packing requiring to be a good fit in the barrel so as to exert a full suction to draw a charge from the tank; and where the pump is enclosed, as is now-a-days often the case, the rider can only tell by the feel when the parts are working properly. A cock is provided at the base of the pump, the handle of which must be turned in one direction (usually horizontally) when drawing oil from the tank, and in another direction (usually downwards) when actuating the plunger for injecting the charge into the crank-case. The frequency of oiling the engine and kindred matters receive attention in a succeeding chapter. It is largely a matter for the individual, and he must use his common-sense as to when the supply should be increased or decreased. Much better over- than under-lubricate, and, best of all, do neither ; but strike a happy medium. Drain off the stale oil from the crank- case at the end of a long run, and always make sure that the oil-retaining screw in the latter is in place and properly screwed home. Should it fall out on the road and the fact be dis- covered, use anything that comes to hand, preferably a cork, to stop up the aperture until a properly fitting plug can be obtained ; otherwise the oil will work out through the open- ing on to the road and be lost for the purpose of lubricating the engine. In fitting a temporary plug, make sure that it clears the flywheels. Periodically the engine should be swilled out with paraffin, and after this has been completely drained off three or four full charges of fresh lubricant should be given.

CHAPTER X.

THE SPRINGING OF MOTOR CYCLES.

THOSE who have never ridden a motor bicycle are apt to allude in tones of disparagement to the "fearful" vibration to which users of that class of machine are, according to them, subjected, and until within the last few years there may have been some point in their criticisms. As in every other direction, however, the springing of the motor cycle has now been very materially improved; but, if there *is* any direction in which the majority of manufacturers have still some opportunity to afford us a wider maximum of comfort, it is in regard to the rear springing; for, although the saddles turned out by the leading firms manufacturing that class of goods are scientifically and beautifully made, it can hardly be said that the ideal has been so nearly approached, where the after part of the machine is concerned, as has been done in connection with spring front forks.

There are several different forms of the latter, most of them efficient, and some superlatively so. What is required in a spring fork is elasticity of movement in the vertical direction, without rolling or sideways action, and this fact is now fully appreciated and provided for in the majority of cases. The front springing must be such as to insulate, so far as is reasonably to be expected, the rider's hands and arms from excessive vibration, even on the roughest roads, without, however, introducing a bouncing or rolling action, and thereby taking away from the ease and stability of the steering. Simplification of construction and moderate cost have also to be considered, but a few makers have not hesitated to provide a spring *frame* as well as spring forks, and, where this is done, the rider's comfort is appreciably added to. The author believes himself to be correct in stating that the spring movement should be in a line approximately with the steering angle, and the rearward movement should increase with the speed of the machine; but for general purposes it may be taken that a fork moves upwards and rearwards at an angle of about 65 to 70 degs.

Compression springs have this advantage over tension springs—that if one breaks it only closes a space equal to the distance between each coil, *i.e.*, about ¼ in. or $\frac{5}{16}$ in. The position of the springs is of the greatest importance. They should be placed in such a position that the shocks are directly absorbed by the inertia of the weight of the

Fig. 118.—The "Truffault" Suspension Spring Fork.

machine. The position of the springs in some forks increases the strain on the latter and the column, instead of relieving it.

The most elaborate spring fork yet applied to a motor bicycle is undoubtedly that known as the Truffault suspension. In this we get a floating action produced by a piston, working in conjunction with a compound spring arrangement inside the steering head. Referring to the drawing (Fig. 118), to the hoop forming part of the front wheel forks is secured

THE SPRINGING OF MOTOR CYCLES. 167

a piston-rod or stem carrying at its upper extremity a plunger, which, as the wheel rises or falls in accordance with the variations in the road surface, works up and down within the steering head of the frame. Above this piston are placed four coiled springs, one within the other, and above these again there is an adjustable stop-piece which may be screwed either in a downward direction to increase the compression of the springs or upwards to release it. In this manner a combined movement of piston and coiled springs is secured, and in front of the head there is provided a guide, or steadying column, with sliding saddle-pieces connected at the bottom to the aforesaid hoop, and which serve to steady and, to some extent, damp the movements of the piston. The author used Truffault forks for a period of upwards of three years on "V.S." motor bicycles and found them admirable in every way. Possibly, the only real objection to them is that it is impossible to use a front wheel brake where they are fitted. The steering appears a little unsteady at first with these forks, but once got used to there is nothing quite so good, from the shock absorbing standpoint, as the Truffault suspension.

FIG. 119.—The "Druid" Spring Forks for Motor Cycles. A much-used type.

Fig. 120.—The "Triumph" Spring Fork.

Fig. 121.—The "A.S.L." Air-Spring Fork.

Fig. 122.—The "Indian" Laminated Spring Fork.

THE SPRINGING OF MOTOR CYCLES. 169

A more simple, but thoroughly efficient, type of spring fork is the "Druid," in which the parallel motion of the forks in relation to the steering column is controlled by means of links pivotally connected to lugs on the steering head, both at top and bottom, and to other lugs brazed on to the forks, these links moving in conjunction with a pair of coiled springs attached to the rear of the main fork. Thus are obtained two rectangles, placed, one at the crown, and the other at the top of the ball-head. The spindles forming the two long sides of the rectangle are firmly fixed in the links forming the two short sides, so that the links do not work upon the spindle ends, but the spindles themselves oscillate in their bearings. As the fork itself is carried on the front portion of these rectangular bearings, it is clear that, as soon as an effort is made to steer the machine,

Fig. 123.—The "Chater-Lea" Spring Fork.

the response of the front wheel must be immediate. The springing effect is admirable, and an advantage of this type is

Fig. 124.
The "Wanderer" Spring Fork, with Tubular Members and Plunger Rods.

Fig 125.—The "Roc" Spring Fork.

that it can be applied—in varying proportions, of course—to practically any motor bicycle, irrespective of horse-power, weight, or other consideration. In some other designs the springs are arranged vertically, just in front of the steering head, and embracing a column forming a part of the fork, there being, in addition, links arranged for pivoted motion and connecting the forks with the steering head.

Fig. 126.—The "Rex" "1910" Spring Fork.

Another example from modern practice is the "Triumph" spring fork, illustrated in Fig. 120. The forks in this design are pivoted on ball-bearings at the crown, which gives a perfectly free motion with only one movable joint, and maintains lateral rigidity (the importance of which has already been emphasised) of the forks.

172   THE MOTOR CYCLIST'S HANDBOOK.

The springs act in a fore and aft direction instead of vertically, as in the previous instances, and the wheel always remains in the same position. Arrangements for adjusting the tension on the springs are provided, and the correct tension is easily ascertained by riding fairly fast on a rough road to see whether vibration is effectively disposed of or not. These forks are fitted exclusively to "Triumph" machines.

Summarised, the points to be aimed at in designing spring front forks for motor cycles are as follows :—

Fig. 127.—The Luxurious Front Springing of the "T.A.C." Four-cylinder Machine.

(1) Absolute lateral rigidity and instant response to steering.
(2) The spring movement should be approximately in line with the steering.
(3) It should allow of the application of a front brake, either band, hub, or rim.
(4) The mudguard should move with the wheel.

(5) The breaking of a spring or springs should not affect the safety of the rider or prevent the machine being ridden.
(6) The easy detachment of the wheel should be provided for.
(7) Shocks should be absorbed without a "galloping" action being set up after passing over an obstruction.
(8) The strain on the steering column should be relieved.

FIG. 128.—Rear Springing of the "T.A.C." Four-cylinder Motor Cycle.

Spring Frames.

On the "Wanderer" and "Bat" motor cycles, and more recently the N.S.U. machines, the frame itself participates in the system of springing. Each of these arrangements is illustrated. In the first instance, the foremost members of the forks are made of tubular section. As the wheel moves upwards or downwards, these tubular members work on

Fig. 129.—The "Bat" Spring Frame.

Fig. 129A.—An 8 h.-p. "Bat" Motor Cycle, with Spring Frame and Forks.

plunger rods, connected with the head, in conjunction with coil springs, as seen in the drawings. The same arrangement is employed at the rear of the frame, and the chain stays are carried at their forward ends on a cross ball-bearing spindle to permit of the springing action taking place. Here also the piston-rod method is combined with coiled springs in compression, and the result is to largely increase the ease and comfort of the rider.

The "Bat" spring frame is illustrated in Fig. 129. The seat column is free to move vertically and independently of the frame. It is held firmly to the latter by four links which are mounted upon ball-bearings. It is then held in position by four spiral springs attached at one end to the frame and at the other to the two top links. Footboards are mounted on the two bottom links. As the rider mounts

Fig. 130.—Diagram of the "N.S.U." Spring Frame for 1911.

the springs gently yield to the varying pressure which his weight produces. The front forks are similarly contrived to isolate the front wheel from the rigid portion of the frame, and the effects produced by unevenness in the road are absorbed by four spiral springs. The front fork ends are provided with adjustable ball-bearings on which an arm carrying the necessary sliding spring holders is mounted and slotted to take the front wheel, and passes entirely round the wheel at the back. The wheel is held rigidly in the horizontal position, but allows free vertical movement; the latter being held in check by the four springs. These springs can be adjusted to any conditions by means of the sliding holders on the arms. In the latest "Bat" machines, the number of front fork springs is reduced to two of larger size. The "N.S.U." spring frame has the chain stays hinged just behind the bottom bracket, and there is a telescopic connection between the bridge of the upper stays and the saddle pillar lug. A strong compression spring surrounds the telescopic member.

FIG. 131.—Another view of the "Wanderer" Spring Fork for Motor Cycles.

Adaptable Springing Devices.

In addition to the springing devices sold integrally with the motor bicycle, there are others supplied by firms of accessory dealers and manufacturers for adaptation to any machine on which rigid forks or other similar out-of-date fittings are employed; as, for instance, old pattern machines which the riders desire to bring up to date. These include spring attachments for the front forks, spring seat pillars, and saddles. The "XL-ALL" specialities of this description are often seen in use, and some of these are included in the appended illustrations.

The Rex Company also provide certain of their more expensive motor bicycles with a cantilever spring saddle support, and a reproduction of this is also given on page 179.

Fig. 132.—The "XL-All" Adaptable Springing Device for Motor Cycle Front Forks.

The A.S.L. firm fits motor bicycles with an air-springing arrangement, comprising a piston moving freely within a cylinder, into which air is introduced to give the necessary resistance and elasticity. This system of springing is adapted for use both at the front and rear portion of the machine. Purchasers of motor cycles should see that the springing arrangements are adequate. As regards saddles, it would be very hard indeed to beat those of Messrs. J. B. Brooks, Ltd., of Birmingham, fitted, as shown in Figs. 135-6 compound coiled springs and padded tops. These saddles are produced with different strengths of spring to accommodate

FIG. 133.—The "N.A.B." Spring Seat Pillar.

different riders' weight, and the whole of the construction is of the highest class. Another very good saddle is the D.L. saddle made by Middlemore & Lamplugh, Ltd., of Coventry. This has twin-tension spiral springs, as shown, with padded leather top to the saddle (Fig. 137).

THE SPRINGING OF MOTOR CYCLES. 179

Fig. 134.—The "Rex" Cantilever Spring Saddle Support.

Fig. 135.—The "Brooks" B-104 Motor Cycle Saddle, with Compound Springs.

Fig. 136.—Compound Springs of "Brooks" Saddle.

Fig. 137.—The Middlemore "D.-L." Saddle.

CHAPTER XI.

Overhauling and Tuning Up the Engine, etc.

When a new motor cycle is delivered to its owner the engine is, or should be, in the pink of condition, and every endeavour should be made to keep it so. Of course, as wear takes place, adjustments become necessary; but it cannot be too repeatedly

Fig. 138.—Overhauling is both interesting and instructive.

or forcibly urged that so long as everything is working properly the best plan is to avoid interference with the maker's adjustments, though it amounts almost to a duty to go carefully over the machine to see that all nuts are properly tightened up.

In the case of a second-hand machine, it may be advisable to overhaul the engine and other parts, with a view to ascertaining their exact condition; but even this may very well be deferred so long as the machine runs well and does what is required of it. It is the author's purpose in the present chapter to deal briefly with the management of the machine, both at home and when out on the road; to briefly consider the more important adjustments and how to make them; and generally to treat of the subject as broadly as is possible in the space at command, from the point of view of those whose knowledge of motor cycle management is either limited or altogether wanting. Some slight reiteration of previously stated points is necessary in places, but this, it is hoped, will be excused in view of the extreme importance of making this portion of our subject especially clear.

Diagnosing Faults.

If the engine is suffering from some definite complaint—such as loss of compression, faulty carburation, or ignition trouble—the symptoms are usually pronounced, and it is possible, as a rule, to rectify the trouble by devoting one's attention entirely to the affected part; but, where general debility is the mischief, a system of " tuning up " all round has to be undertaken, and this may involve the overhauling of several vital organs in turn, each one of which has become lacking in its ability to properly perform its allotted function. And then, again, it is not necessary to wait for the development of a fault before undertaking an important adjustment. The careful motor cyclist always takes a good look round his machine before setting out on a ride of any length, and in this way he often detects—and puts right in the shed before starting—something which, had it been neglected until out on the road, might have caused delay and bother, and which, in any case, could be more conveniently dealt with at home.

The Maintenance of Power.

The makers design their engines to develop a certain horse-power at a given speed in revolutions per minute, and anything below that speed means a lowering of the horse-power at disposal. Therefore, it must always be the endeavour of the owner to maintain the ability of his engine to reach the necessary speed to give its maximum horse-power when required, and unless all vital parts are working efficiently it is impossible to secure this happy result. A sound frame, comfortable saddle, and efficient tyres, are all highly necessary to the success of motor cycling ; but given these, and at the same time a poorly conditioned engine, very little real pleasure can be obtained from the use of the machine, and the whole thing becomes a source of anxiety and trouble, and, maybe, expense into the bargain. How necessary, therefore, that every motor cyclist should think and act for himself in the maintenance of his machine, and not have to go

Fig. 139.—The "Compression" escapes wherever it can find the smallest outlet.

running to the repairer for every little adjustment and for the rectification of every little fault as it arises.

The Fit of Piston Rings.

To begin with, there cannot be speed and power unless the *compression* is good. Therefore, see that the piston rings are a good springy fit in their grooves, without vertical play

OVERHAULING THE ENGINE. 183

therein, but able to expand and form a gastight contact with the walls of the cylinder. If the petrol gas is enabled to escape past the piston rings to any appreciable extent, the fact will be denoted by the appearance on the rings of discolourations resembling burns, and this should be taken as a sure index of loss of compression. The remedy is to replace the ring or rings with other and better fitting ones, and the opportunity should be embraced while the grooves are free to clean them, as if the engine has been working for

FIG 140.—How to remove Piston Rings without breaking them.

some time without attention, accumulations of carbonised oil will be found adhering to them and this interferes with the fit of the rings. To remove the piston rings it is a good plan to cut three pieces of tin, about 1 in. wide, and insert these at regular distances around the piston, and between it and the rings. The latter can then be worked off gently by the fingers without fear of breakage, and the same plan can be resorted to when replacing the rings or fitting new ones, although, generally speaking, it is easier and less risky to fit rings on than to take them off. Until the new piston rings have "worked themselves in," the compression will in all probability remain faulty. A hundred-mile run will, however, put matters right in this direction.

Piston rings are made of cast-iron, and are, therefore, easily broken. They cost from 1/- to as much as 1/6 each; so that it is just as well to be careful in handling them. Some engines have "stepped" rings (see Fig. 38), the slots being undercut, and, in some designs, a small pin is inserted in the groove so that rotation of the ring in its groove is prevented. Care is necessary with the ordinary type of ring with diagonally cut slots to see that the slots do not lie in the same vertical plane when replacing the cylinder, for if this occurs,

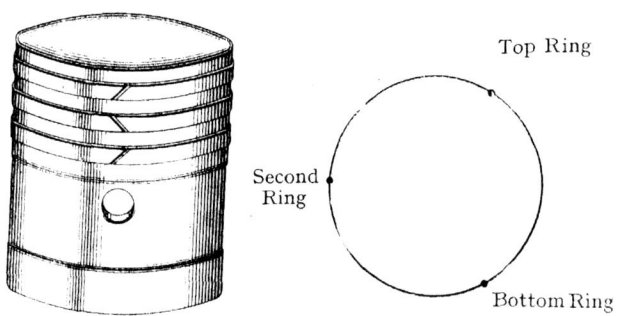

Fig. 141.—The wrong way of setting the Piston Ring Slots.   The right way.

there is likely to be some loss of compression; but all the care in the world will not prevent their sometimes *working* into line of their own accord while the engine is running, if they are at all a slack fit. With the stepped and pinned type of piston ring, illustrated in a previous chapter, this cannot, of course, occur. After a very large amount of use has been made of the engine—say, at the end of some 40,000 miles or more—it may become advisable to re-bore the cylinder and fit a new piston and rings. There is a tendency for the cylinder to lose its parallel bore after long usage, and when this has occurred nothing will ensure a good compression except the aforesaid measures, and this, of course, is a job for a competent mechanic alone.

Grinding in the Valves.

Having made sure that the piston rings are both well fitting and properly aligned, the next point towards maintaining a good compression is to keep the inlet and exhaust valves properly ground into their seats so that leakage cannot take place there either. The exhaust valve is naturally the chief offender in this respect, for it has to withstand the constant passage, between its surface and the seating, of burnt

FIG. 142.—Special Tool for grinding Motor Cycle Engine Valves.

gases at a very high temperature and velocity, whereas the inlet valve only has clean, unburnt gas to deal with, which, as a matter of fact, imparts a certain amount of lubricating influence to the valve. The action of the exhaust gases is to produce, in course of time, abrasions and pit-markings on the exhaust valve and its seating, and when this has occurred to any marked degree the ability of the valve and seating to prevent leakage of the gas past them during the compression stroke is impaired and may become seriously so if the grinding operation is not undertaken.

It is a very easy matter to grind in an ordinary mechanical valve—all that is necessary being to remove the spring and cotter, smear a mixture of oil and emery, or other prepared powder, such as carborundum, on its surface, and then rotate the valve in its seating, either by means of a screwdriver or a brace, until both the surface of the valve and the seating which receives it are freed from pit-marks and both present a smooth, even surface all round. At the same time, this is just one of those matters which require doing *properly* to get the best results. The valve must, during the grinding operation, be lifted at intervals and allowed to assume a different position in the seating, and the grinding medium must be renewed from time to time as the work proceeds.

FIG. 143.—Valve Spring Lifter. Useful when removing or replacing a Mechanical Valve.

It is a good plan to place a weak spring—as, for instance, an old A.O.I. valve spring—under the head of the valve, so that directly the pressure on the screwdriver or other instrument is relaxed, the valve will rise automatically, and can be either lifted out or rotated slightly as the operator desires. Many motor cyclists make special grinding tools for themselves, and the author has found the one illustrated in Fig. 142 very useful for the purpose. Continuous grinding in one position often produces ridges on valve and seating, and may quite possibly make matters worse than they were at first. It is sometimes a difficult job to get the spring and cotter free when setting out to do valve grinding. Special tools are sold for this purpose (Fig. 143), and the few shillings they cost probably repay the purchaser in the long run, if only by saving the cost of sticking plaster for barked knuckles. Always place a piece of rag in the port opening while grinding in a valve in order to prevent even the smallest particle of the abrasive grinding mixture from entering the cylinder.

The "Lift" of M.O. Valves.

The next point—and a *very* important one—is the maintenance of a proper gap or space between the bottom of the valve stem and the face of the tappet which operates it. In course of time the valve stem wears and shortens, and the gap is then increased, so that the valve does not receive its full opening. Mechanical valves require about $\frac{1}{4}$-in. lift off their seats, that representing, in the case of an average valve, about one quarter of the effective diameter. The timing-gear cam and other parts are designed to provide this amount of

FIG. 144.—There should be just sufficient space for a visiting card to pass between the Valve Stem and Tappet with engine cold.

opening, but the tendency is, of course, for it to become less as wear takes place. The space between valve stem and tappet should be just sufficient to allow a visiting card of ordinary thickness to be passed, not *forced*, through with engine cold; and this being so, when the valve heats up and the stem slightly expands, the gap will be, to a very small extent, reduced and the full valve lift assured.

When the valve stem has worn and the space is consequently increased, matters may be rectified either by brazing an extension-piece on the stem and then filing down to the exact length required, or other means of effecting the same result may be employed. When the tappets themselves have become markedly worn they should be replaced by others, and here the cost is a very moderate one. The cams only require renewing at long intervals, a huge mileage being usually put up before any such measure becomes necessary as the result of wear. A few makers fit their engines with adjustable tappets, and, provided the locking arrangements on these are well designed, the idea has much to commend it. If not, or the workmanship and fitting are not of the best, trouble may ensue, as the result of the tappet automatically adjusting itself when not required.

A new valve will generally be found to possess too long a stem, and it is highly necessary that this should be cut to [*exactly* the right length, for it is easy to see that if the length be only ever so slightly in excess of what is correct, the stem and tappet will be brought permanently in contact and the valve will be prevented from bedding into its seat. A definite loss of compression will be the result, and it may be even impossible to start the engine at all. If, on the other hand, the stem is shortened too much, the evil previously described will arise.

The exhaust valve lifting mechanism sometimes provides a means of difficulty, especially for the embryo motor cyclist. Care must be taken to see that the lifting lever (or whatever form of device is employed for raising the valve) lies clear of the tappet at all other times than when deliberately brought into contact therewith by the rider at starting or otherwise in the course of manipulating the engine.

Valve Springs.

Loss of engine speed may arise from using springs of insufficient strength on mechanically-operated valves. The beginner should never experiment in this direction, but should consult the makers of the engine if he has any reason to believe that inefficiency is arising from this cause. Too *strong* a spring, on the other hand, may result in valve breakage by bringing the valve down with undue force on its seating. It is very necessary that valves should be smartly and promptly closed at the proper times, but sledge-hammer methods are certainly *not* wanted.

Adjusting A.O.I. Valves.

The adjustments necessary in the case of an automatic valve are, perhaps, more easily carried into effect than where

OVERHAULING THE ENGINE. 189

the valve is of the M.O. type; but, at the same time, they require more delicate handling, as only a very slight variation makes a tremendous difference in the running of the engine, especially a twin-cylinder one. Some A.O.I. valves are secured, with their springs, by means of the cup and cotter method, much the same as in a mechanical valve; but, in others, the stem of the valve is screw-threaded and locknuts are employed for varying the tension on the spring. Both methods are illustrated in Fig. 145. The valve should be given a lift of about $\frac{1}{32}$-in. at the start and this, in course of working, will automatically increase to $\frac{1}{8}$ in., and more, if left for long periods without attention. A simple method of reducing the opening of the valve where the cotter method of fixing is employed is to place a washer, as shown in the drawing, on the column surrounding the stem, and with which

FIG. 145.—Two methods of securing and adjusting A.O.I. Valves.
(See accompanying description.)

the collar comes into contact as the valve opens, thus limiting the travel of the valve. With the lock-nut method, as shown in the second sketch, adjustments are easily effected by screwing the nuts in one direction or the other to give more or less valve opening as may be desired. As was pointed out in a previous chapter, a small automatic valve opening increases the speed of the engine, while a larger opening reduces it, but makes it possible to run the engine, firing regularly, at low speeds. If the opening be really excessive, what is known as "blowing-back" in the carburettor may occur. The inlet valves at such times admit more gas than the engine can take, and a portion of the charge is forced to return to the carburettor. This prevents the supply of suitable mixture being maintained, interfering with the action of the carburettor and the proper working of the engine. Automatic inlet valves practically never require grinding in, and when they do, the task is the easiest one imaginable, owing to the fact that the seating comes away from the engine with the valve. It is very necessary in a twin-cylinder engine that both A.O.I. valves should have precisely the same amount of opening and springs of identical strength, and a good way to secure this is to press the stems of the two valves against one another (each valve being complete with spring and seating), and the valve which opens first shows itself to have a weaker spring than the other, and must, if the other valve is getting a correct opening, be provided with a rather stronger spring, so that when pressing against its mate both open simultaneously with identical adjustments.

Fig. 146.—Testing Automatic Inlet Valves for opening.

Cylinder, etc., Jointings.

All jointings—such as where the valve caps, sparking plug, and compression tap screw into the cylinder—must be made compression tight by interposing copper and asbestos washers, and to test these engine oil may be smeared around the joints, and the engine pedalled or otherwise turned over compression, when, if there is any leakage, it will show itself by the appearance of tiny bubbles caused by the escape through the oil film of the air or gas under compression. The task of removing the sparking plug, valve caps, etc., is sometimes fraught with difficulty, owing to the parts having become so tightly fixed in their places by reason of the heat they are subjected to, that they cannot be loosened. Use a properly fitting " fixed " spanner and, if very obstinate, the parts should be well soaked with paraffin and then left for a while before again attempting to loosen them. A sharp blow on the end of the spanner with a hammer may be necessary.

Carbonised Deposits.

Before leaving that part of our subject which deals with the care of the piston, cylinder, valves, etc., a few words may be added as to the necessity of removing the carbonised deposits which will be found both on the inside and outside of the piston head, the combustion chamber of the cylinder and other parts, when the cylinder has been removed. A clearance of these deposits is recommended at the end of every 1,500 miles (the author himself, who believes in rather overdoing than underdoing the lubricating of the engine, takes the job in hand, on the average, every 1,000 miles), and believes it to be beneficial and wholly worth while. If heavy accumulations of burnt oil, road dust, and whatever the other constituents may be, are left on the parts, a tendency to pre-ignition is induced, owing to the gases being fired by incandescent effect before the electric spark is timed to take place, and back-firing—*i.e.*, explosions, occurring before the piston is in a suitable position—results. The engine tends also to overheat, and, in any case, it is not working under anything like such healthy conditions as when the parts are clean. The accumulations are easily chipped away by the aid of a screwdriver or other blunt instrument, the whole job occupying but ten minutes or a quarter of an hour at most, after access has been gained to the parts.

When clearing the top of the piston, it is well to stuff a piece of rag into the crank-case opening so that the burnt matter cannot fall through the latter and get mixed up with the lubricating oil when the engine is subsequently working. Some motor cyclists smear the top of the piston with graphite, with the idea of preventing, in some measure, the collection of carbon deposits, but it is doubtful whether they gain much by so doing.

Removing and Replacing the Cylinder.

Before removing the cylinder of a motor cycle engine, it is a good plan to squirt a few drops of paraffin or petrol through the compression tap. This will free the piston and simplify the task of getting the cylinder off. Take the cylinder in both hands and, having previously moved the piston to the bottom of the stroke by means of the pulley, partly rotate the cylinder backwards and forwards on the piston, while at the same time pulling upwards. Different engines require different treatment and, in some, the best way to get the cylinder clear is to place the connecting-rod and piston at an acute angle fore or aft of the crank-case, so that more space is available than when the latter parts are vertical and the cylinder has to be lifted up directly underneath the tank (see Fig. 147 below).

FIG. 147.—Removing the Cylinder. Arrows indicate the direction of successive movements.

When replacing the cylinder, make sure that the jointing material between it and the crank-case is in good condition; if not, it must be replaced by a fresh one. Before doing this, however, make sure that the two surfaces are clean and smooth. An efficient jointing can be made of brown paper soaked in oil, and, in preparing this, first cut a disc out to allow of the paper sheet being passed over the piston, and then shape out the jointing (and the four holes for the holding

OVERHAULING THE ENGINE. 193

FIG. 148.—Making a Cylinder Jointing by the "Template" method.

FIG. 149.—The complete 'Arno$_1$' Power Unit.
Detached sideways from the frame *en bloc* in a few minutes by
removing two bolts at front and two at rear.

down screws to pass through) by means of light tapping with a hammer. The work of cutting out a jointing with scissors is tedious and unnecessary. Remember, that if the thickness of the jointing is materially increased, it will tend to raise the cylinder and may interfere, if carried too far, with the gap between the tappet and valve stems. In some engines it is impracticable to remove the cylinder alone; the whole engine has to be taken down. In a case like the "Arno" (Fig. 149), where four bolts placed vertically in *horizontal* bracket connections secure the engine in the frame, it is a very easy matter to remove or replace it single-handed. But in most designs, directly the engine is taken out the downtube members of the frame "whip in," and the replacement of the engine becomes a "two-man job"—and not an easy one at that.

Tuning up the Carburettor.

Carburettor adjustments are necessarily rather delicate ones and need careful consideration at times. There is, however, no part of the mechanism associated with a motor cycle engine which should be spared the attentions of the inexperienced (sometimes rudely described as "tinkering") so much as this one. If the level of the petrol is practically flush with the top of the jet, with the machine resting on both wheels and the carburettor fixed in its running position, and the needle valve forms a good joint in its seating, the proper sizes of jet and choke tube (or adapter) are fitted, and intelligent use is made of the extra air lever, matters will be found to be about right. Guidance in the direction of selecting the proper sizes of jet and adapter for particular engine powers was given in the Chapter on "The Carburettor," and it is an easy matter with modern carburettors to experiment one size larger or one smaller if the engine shows a desire either for more or less air when running under normal conditions.

The motor cyclist must be guided by the symptoms displayed by his engine, and not rush, as the majority do, to the immediate assumption that the carburettor is responsible directly there is any falling off of power. Any interruption in the supply of fuel to the engine will naturally bring about erratic working, and perhaps a total stoppage; but this may arise from other causes, among them being ignition failures and other temporary derangements.

Needle Valve Adjustments.

If the needle valve is a poor fit in its seat, overflowing of the petrol may result. Sometimes a little piece of grit gets lodged in the seating under the valve and, this removed, matters assume their wonted condition. Then small particles of matter get lodged in the jet and partially stop up the bore, thus impeding or altogether stopping the flow of petrol. The rider should first ascertain that neither of these things have happened before he undertakes more drastic remedies. A few motor bicycles are fitted with petrol strainers designed to prevent the ingress of any particle of foreign matter in the petrol to the carburettor. The level of petrol in the jet can be adjusted by means of the brass collar on the needle valve; if the position of this collar is lowered on the needle it effects the *raising* of the petrol level, but if it be lifted higher up on the needle the level will *drop*. Overflowing occurs when the petrol level is too high, and starving of the engine when it is too low. Underneath the cover of the carburettor float chamber will be found the two balance weights previously mentioned. Removal of the split pins holding these will liberate the needle carrying the collar (the latter being driven tightly in place but otherwise permitting of movement), and it is an easy matter to shift the position of the collar by lightly tapping it with a hammer, the needle itself being preferably held in a vice. A very small adjustment makes a lot of difference, and the needle should be marked before anything is done, as an indication of what the original position was.

Difficulty in Starting.

If difficulty in starting the engine is experienced, and the ignition and other parts are known to be in perfectly good order, with the piston working freely in the cylinder, it may be that too much air is being admitted to the spraying chamber of the carburettor, thus weakening the mixture below explosion point at slow speeds when the magneto spark is weakest, and as a test a smaller adapter should be fitted. Raising of the petrol level (if below top of jet) may effect an improvement, or a larger jet may be needed. On the other hand, it may be wholly due to faulty manipulation of the levers, and experiments with varying positions of these will generally show which are the best to secure good behaviour at starting. Some engines require a fairly full throttle opening and the extra air shut right off; others will not start unless extra air is admitted, while others again require some different setting. Usually throttle one-third open and extra air closed is about right.

In cases of partial or total stoppage, the first thing to do, before blaming the carburettor itself, is to make sure that there *is* petrol in the tank, and that it is getting through without impediment to the carburettor. Disconnect the petrol pipe union from the base of the float chamber and turn on the tap near tank, and if the flow is not a full one remove the pipe altogether and seek for the cause. Also make sure that the garage man didn't give you water instead of petrol (this happened once to the author) by allowing a small quantity to flow on to the ground or other flat surface, and if it quickly evaporates all is right. Always use a funnel fitted with a fine wire gauze strainer that will retain water but allow petrol to pass when filling the tank up. A piece of muslin will do as a makeshift. Ascertain if any leakage is going on between the tank and the carburettor, at the petrol unions or around the junction of the pipe with the tank, and endeavour to trace the cause of the trouble from its source onwards to its discovery. If the extra air orifice of the carburettor is fitted with a gauze covering make sure that this is kept clean. If choked with dust the air cannot get through, and faulty running may result.

Ignition Faults.

Faults connected with the ignition (or, perhaps, it would be fairer to say: their predisposing causes) are numerous. They may be due to failure on the part of the accumulator or magneto to produce a sufficiently intense current, or the defect may arise somewhere between the generating medium and the point at which the electricity performs its function of igniting the charge. The high tension cable or its connections may require attention or renewal, the sparking plug be amiss, or the contact-breaker have developed a fault which is preventing the engine from working. The usual *modus operandi* is to first test the accumulator, coil (page 114) or magneto to discover whether the current is being generated properly. The accumulator should show 4·5 by voltmeter, or, if the lamp

OVERHAULING THE ENGINE. 197

FIG. 150.—Testing an Accumulator by the lamp method.

test be applied, a bright light should be obtained, and the magneto, when tested by means of the small appliance provided for the purpose, should produce a bright electric spark. The appliance referred to is a small spanner with spring opening at the centre, which can be "snapped" on to the high-tension terminal in such a way that its two ends are each close to the inside of the magneto, as seen in Fig. 151. With the spanner in this position the armature should be rotated by using the pedalling gear or wheeling the machine along the road, the timing lever being set at full advance beforehand. If the magneto itself is in proper working condition the spark will occur, and the fault must be sought either in the cable or sparking plug, and, as a matter of fact, the sparking plug is usually the first thing examined.

If, however, no spark appears, the contact-breaker must be inspected to see whether the platinum points are properly making and breaking contact. When the fibre block passes out of the recess, the distance between the platinum points should be 0·5 mm. Should this not be so, the points must be adjusted by means of the screws provided for the purpose. Should, however, the amount of "break" be correct, the best plan is to remove the contact-

FIG. 151.—Testing the current at the Magneto. (A) Spanner, (B) Carbon Holder and High-tension Terminal, (C) Magnets. Arrow indicates direction of spark across air gap

breaker disc altogether by unscrewing the retaining screw, and if the platinum points are found to be dirty or pitted, they must be touched up with a smooth file or fine emery cloth until quite clean, making an even contact. The contact-breaker and the parts connected with it should always be kept quite clean (petrol is useful here) as nothing tends to interfere with their working more than an accumulation of oil and dirt. In the case of the new pattern single-cylinder Bosch magnetos, in which, as before described, the snap on terminal has been discarded in favour of the water-tight carbon-holder illustrated on page 95, the method of testing is as follows :—

The conducting wire should first be detached from the magneto and a fresh wire put into the carbon-holder and brought into such a position as to leave a distance of 1 mm. between its end and the magneto. Set the timing lever to position of full advance, and rotate the magneto by pedalling the machine. If a powerful spark passes regularly between the magneto and the end of the wire, it is clear that the magneto itself is in working order, and the fault must be looked for in the cable or sparking plug.

If the fault is in the cable, it may be detected by attaching the latter to the magneto in the manner provided, and holding the opposite end so that the brass terminal piece intended for connection with the sparking plug nearly touches the cylinder or other metal object. Now again rotate the engine by the pedals, and if the cable is alright, a spark will jump across the gap between the terminal and the cylinder. If it does not, there is something which requires remedying, and most likely it will be a loose terminal, broken or frayed wires, or the insulation of the cable may have somewhere in its length have been destroyed. Next, to test the sparking plug, attach to it the cable and adopt the same method as when testing the cable. If a good spark jumps from plug to cylinder, well and good ; if not, examine plug and find out what is wrong. Perhaps one of the points is touching the central electrode, thus short-circuiting the current; or a speck of foreign matter has become lodged between the two, thus bringing about the same result ; or, the porcelain insulation may be broken and loose, the points covered with oil, or other derangements have arisen. It is generally possible to repair the mischief, but the best plan

OVERHAULING THE ENGINE.

by far is to change the plug for another (no experienced motor cyclist ever goes out without a spare plug at his disposal) and defer the setting of matters to rights in the affected plug until a more convenient occasion. Sometimes in very wet and dirty weather the working of the magneto may be interrupted by water gaining access to the interior of the machine; but, fortunately, this does not often happen. Short-circuiting also occurs at times as a result of wet on the high-tension terminal and cable connections; but where the magneto is carried at the back of the cylinder under the tank or a protective cover is used, these things cannot very well happen. Neither can they where the water-tight carbon-holders are in use, and those who are not fortunate enough to possess these may secure

FIG. 152.—Testing the High-tension Cable.

FIG. 153.—Testing the Sparking Plug.

reasonable immunity by liberally smearing the terminals with vaseline in wet weather. A stuck-up A.O.I. valve will prevent the engine starting, and the plunger provided for the purpose should be depressed with the finger to free the valve from its seat.

Testing the Ignition Adjustments.

The readers' attention has already been called to the adjustments necessary to ensure a suitable timing of the magneto spark in relation to the movements of the piston, and the drawing Fig. 72, on page 99 of the chapter on Ignition,

200 THE MOTOR CYCLIST'S HANDBOOK.

was designed to assist him in undertaking the task for himself. When the timing of the ignition has been completed it serves a useful purpose (as a test) to run the engine on the stand and note the exact results pro-

FIG. 154.—Wedges between Pulley and Crank-case assist in getting Pulley loosened for removal.

FIG. 155.—The Pulley should by this means come away quite easily.

FIG. 156.—An easily-made and efficient Pulley Shifter.

duced by working the timing lever on the tank very gradually from position of maximum advance to that of maximum retard and, in the author's experience, the adjustment is correct when the engine will continue regularly firing at full retard, and the throttle is set in normal position for running full advanced on the level under load—*i.e.*, about one-third open, with air to suit. It will then be found, with most engines, that full advance can be given without any fear of causing the engine to knock, and as the sparking lever is brought slowly from retard to advance, the speed of the engine will rapidly increase up to the last fraction of movement, and it is not necessary to open the throttle wider to get the engine to continue firing when maximum retard is reached. Should the engine run faster when *almost* fully advanced than when a*ctually* fully advanced, it shows conclusively that too much advance has been given and the gear or chain drive must be set back slightly in the opposite direction to that in which the contact-breaker of the magneto revolves—that is, in the direction of retard.

The Engine Pulley.

The pulley is secured on the engine shaft by means of a key and keyway, and also by nuts on the end of the shaft. If these nuts work loose the full brunt of the work of retaining the pulley in place falls on the key and should the nuts fall off on to the road the pulley will not be long in following them. These nuts should be occasionally tested with a spanner to ascertain whether any tightening up is required. The pulley may be removed from the engine shaft after removing the nuts by placing screwdrivers or wedges between it and the crank-case and then dealing some smart, but not heavy, blows with a hammer on the end of the shaft. Leave a nut slightly overhanging the shaft when doing this or else hold a block of hard wood between hammer and end of shaft to avoid injuring the screw threads on the latter.

The Brakes.

The brakes on a motor cycle may be of several different types. The law insists on each machine having two brakes, each capable of locking the wheel, and the majority of up-to-date machines are equipped with a brake on each wheel, that on the front one being applied by Bowden mechanism and acting on both sides of the rim, while the rear wheel brake is foot-applied and acts on the belt rim. Some makers employ a band brake on one side of the rear wheel and a rim brake on the other; but the better plan is to distribute the braking effect over both wheels. Particular attention should be given by every motor cyclist to the condition of his brakes, as failure on the part of either may bring about an accident, while, should both be in a defective condition, the consequences may prove fatal either to the rider or some other user of the highway.

Fig. 157.—Band Brake for the Rear Wheel of a Motor Bicycle.

Fig. 158.—Belt Rim Brake for Motor Cycles. A popular and efficient type.

Care of the Bicycle Parts, etc.

The wheels, pedalling gear, free-wheel, steering head, and other "bicycle" parts should receive regular attention, as well as the engine, their lubrication being regularly attended to, and any adjustments necessary should be made without undue delay. The tyres require looking after, bad cuts should be stopped with a tyre filling, and an occasional look round the outer covers may lead to the discovery and removal of what might otherwise provide a means of puncturing the tyre during the next ride. Loose spokes should be put right as soon as possible after detection ; and, in short, a careful watch should be kept on every part of the construction. Keep the *outside* of the engine as clean as possible, using a stiff brush dipped in paraffin or waste petrol, so that accumulations of mud and grease can be removed from the most inaccessible parts. A dirty, neglected-looking engine is always a bad recommendation to the user, and, what is more, the cooling is in a measure retarded. When a grease-covered crank-case gets thoroughly warmed up, the odour given off from it is a very unpleasant one.

Methods of Starting.

With each and all of the foregoing engine adjustments properly attended to, there should be no difficulty in starting at the first attempt. It is advisable, especially during cold weather, to inject a little paraffin and petrol mixed, through the compression tap into the cylinder so that the piston rings, between which and the cylinder walls a film of thick oil is deposited when the engine is stationary, may be freed from its " gummed up " position.

To effect starting of the engine, apart from the machine as a whole, the back wheel should be jacked up off the ground by means of the stand provided for that purpose, the petrol turned on, carburettor flooded by depressing the plunger on float chamber, spark lever well, but not fully advanced, and the throttle opened from one-third to one-half with the extra air either closed entirely, or, in some cases, slightly opened. Raise the exhaust valve lifter and smartly pedal the engine round, dropping the exhaust lifter directly a fair speed has been got on the engine—*i.e.*, after two or three turns of the pedals. The engine should at once fire and, if the owner is a novice, he will be well advised to acquaint himself with the manipulation of the various levers, etc., before venturing out for his first ride. On no account whatever should he keep the engine running for more than half a minute at a time on the stand, as, in these circumstances, it is deprived entirely of the cooling effects which it obtains when out on the road, and will get very hot if made to continue running under such conditions. A pumpful of oil may be given with advantage during the stationary test,

CHAPTER XII.

THE MACHINE AS A WHOLE—THE SELECTION AND PURCHASE OF NEW AND SECOND-HAND MACHINES—DRIVING HINTS—PASSENGER MOTOR CYCLES—THE COST OF MOTOR CYCLING.

IN the preceding chapters the author has endeavoured to explain the construction and functions of the various parts of a motor cycle and the engine which propels it. Also the principal adjustments necessary to keep the machine in proper working order, and so forth, and by this means it is hoped that the reader will have acquired sufficient insight

FIG. 159.—The "Moto-Rêve" 2 h.-p. Single-cylinder Lightweight Motor Bicycle.

into the subject to enable him to discern what is requisite in the completed machine, and to be able to judge somewhat of the differences which exist between one type and another.

The average purchaser of a motor bicycle has a fairly big proposition to deal with, unless, for one reason or another, he be possessed of means or is able to decide off-hand exactly which make of machine he will favour. The man who, knowing little or nothing of the subject, decides to become a motor cyclist, is, as a rule, led first one way and then the other by the advice of friends or the blandishments of the makers' representatives; and in the end it may quite well come about that he buys a machine, not so much because of his own inclinations in the matter as because of the wonderful qualities others have assured him it possesses. He may quite possibly profit by the advice he gets, and secure thereby a motor cycle which will serve him faithfully and well for a very considerable time; but, on the other hand, he is just as likely to acquire either an unsuitable or an inferior make, and be led by the consequences to give up the pastime altogether.

FIG. 160.—The "Moto-Rêve" Twin-cylinder Lightweight, $2\frac{3}{4}$ h.-p.

The prospective motor cyclist should, therefore, look well into the matter before he parts with his money—by all means consulting those who know more about it than he does—but reserving the summing up and final judgment to himself after mature deliberation. A motor bicycle costs a fair sum of money, and to suitably equip it with accessories, pay licensing and other fees, and generally set up as "a motorist in a small way," and then discover that another make would have met his particular requirements much better, is, to say the least, disheartening, and likely, as before intimated, to make one "give up the game" altogether.

The Question of Type and First Cost.

The first thing to be considered is—what can the intending purchaser afford to expend, and, that decided, which *class* (as apart from make) of machine will best conform to his requirements? If the beginner is of moderate physique and pecuniary resources, he may do best to invest in a good second-hand light (or medium) weight machine, with engine power ranging from 2 to 3 h.-p., which will take him almost anywhere he is likely to want to go, and do the work cheaply in respect of petrol and oil consumption, wear of tyres and general upkeep. If, however, he be fairly well set up in both respects and entertains a preference for something more powerful, a $3\frac{1}{2}$ h.-p. bicycle with heavier tyres, greater weight, and costing rather more to maintain, will, perhaps, be more suitable for all round use.

Fig. 101.—The "Hobart" $2\frac{1}{4}$ h.-p. Lightweight Motor Bicycle.

Where expense is not such an important matter and the rider can afford to pick and choose from among the best motor cycles, he will doubtless make his choice of a brand new machine, with such refinements as may appear to him desirable. It depends very much upon the nature of the work to be performed, the financial position of the purchaser, his temperament and capabilities.

If a lot of heavy work is to be done—*i.e.*, riding in difficult country with a bulky outfit, going out in all weathers and wherever business or pleasure takes one—it is advisable to have power and plenty of it; and to obtain really good results it may be desirable to purchase a machine fitted with a free engine clutch or two-speed gear. It is difficult enough to offer advice in such a matter as this, for there are so many individual preferences and considerations to be taken into account that it becomes almost impossible to lay down any system, let alone a definite law, to be followed by the novice, or, for the matter of that, by the more experienced motor cyclist either.

Avoid Unnecessary Weight and Excessive Engine Power.

One thing, however, may be urged with conviction, and that is, that no one, not possessed of average activity and strength, should burden themselves with a heavy, high-powered, complicated machine, far in excess both as regards engine capacity and weight, of their requirements, and needing an extra lot of looking after to keep in good

FIG. 162.—The Lady's $2\frac{1}{2}$ h.-p. "Hobart."

order. At all other times than when the rider is being carried along by it, and sometimes even then the handling of such a machine inflicts a heavy tax on the resources of its possessor. The strong and youthful, or comparatively youthful, reader will probably disagree with these remarks and contend that there is "nothing like" a 7 h.-p. twin, which will roar up any hill you like to put it at and jib at nothing to be met with on the roads of this country; but in time he, too, will come round to a saner way of viewing the matter and be content with a lighter, cheaper, and altogether handier mount, which can be used for almost any purpose and worked within a reasonable distance of its power capacity most of the time, instead of some 50 per cent. of the engine power developed going to waste practically all the time, besides other disadvantages.

Where the intention is to employ a side car and take an extra passenger *frequently*, it is not only advisable, but indispensable, to employ a powerful engine, set in a strong and heavy frame, and, further than this, to utilise a variable speed gear, and if (as before remarked) real touring and the adoption of the "go anywhere and do anything" principle is contemplated ; but, unless this be the case, the purchaser will be much better advised to modify his tastes and go in for something of lighter build.

The beginner may well be pardoned if he fails to under-

FIG. 163.—The "Hobart" $3\frac{1}{2}$ h.-p. Twin-cylinder Motor Bicycle.

stand how it is that so many engines, with differently proportioned cylinders, can be described as of the same horsepower. His best plan will be not to worry about the point, for practically all motor cycle engines develop a greater horsepower than the makers claim for them.

The R.A.C. (Royal Automobile Club) has provided a simple formula for calculating the approximate horse-power of motor-car and cycle engines, as follows :—

$$\text{R.A.C.} \quad \text{H.P.} = \frac{D^2 \times N}{2 \cdot 5}$$

when stroke is taken into consideration.

$$\text{H.P.} = \frac{D \times S \times N}{2 \cdot 5}$$

MANAGEMENT OF THE MOTOR CYCLE.

where D = diameter of cylinder in inches.
,,   S = stroke of piston in inches.
,,   N = number of cylinders.

And to ascertain the cubic capacity of the cylinder the most simple plan is to square the bore of cylinder × ·7854 × stroke.

Second-hand Motor Cycles.

It is a good plan for the absolute novice to commence operations by purchasing a second- or third-hand machine, with which to serve his novitiate as a motor cyclist. A really good and fairly modern machine can be picked up for a moderate sum—say, £16 to £20, and many for considerably

FIG. 164.—2¾-3 h.-p. " Arno " Motor Bicycle, with Ball-bearing Engine, *as ridden by the Author*.

less than this, being of older pattern ; but it is necessary that the beginner should go exceedingly carefully to work, or he may find himself landed with a machine of little worth until a further sum has been expended in putting it into working order. If he numbers motor cyclists among his friends, he should prevail upon one or more of them to go along with him to inspect the proffered mount ; but, if this is impossible, he may adopt one or two simple precautions as a guard against being misled by an unscrupulous, or too enthusiastic, vendor.

Inspection before Purchase.

The compression of the engine should be tested by standing on the pedal, with rear wheel jacked up clear of the ground, and at least several secondss hould elapse before the weight of the person making the test forces the engine round over compression. If there are no pedals, wheel the machine along the ground with belt on and exhaust-lifter released, when, if the compression be in order, the back wheel will skid as the piston travels upward towards the end of the compression stroke. Examine the pulley shaft for wear, taking hold of the pulley itself and seeing whether there is any *vertical* movement. If there is to any appreciable degree, it may be taken as evidence of the fact that the engine shaft, and most probably other bearings, also require re-bushing, and this should weigh very considerably in the mind of the prospective purchaser and go far towards deciding him whether or not to go any further in the matter.

FIG. 165.—3½ h.-p. " Arno " Motor Bicycle, with Ball-bearing engine.
A powerful model of sound design and construction.

The condition of the ignition apparatus, whether accumulator or magneto system, should be closely investigated, and anyone who has taken the trouble to read the foregoing explanations in the Chapter on Ignition, should be able to tell within a little whether these appliances on a second-hand motor bicycle are in reasonably good order or not. Next, it is advisable to inspect the general state of the engine, noting whether any part of the radiating fins have been broken off the cylinder, or other signs of rough or negligent treatment exist. If the previous owner has been careless or unfortunate in these respects, the still more important interior parts may have suffered equally in his hands, and the exterior condition of the machine may generally be taken in some respects as an index of the condition of affairs inside.

The frame, wheels, and other "bicycle" parts should be looked over, loose spokes or other likely faults, if possible, detected, and pointed out to the seller, while the make and condition of the tyres should be especially noted. The price asked should depend in some measure upon what accessories are included in the bargain, how old the machine is, and what amount of mileage it would appear to have covered. The owner's estimate of this latter point plus (in most cases) some 50 per cent., may be taken as representing something near the truth.

FIG. 166.—The "Douglas" $2\frac{3}{4}$ h.-p. Motor Bicycle, with horizontally-opposed Cylinders and Two-speed Gear.

Above all, insistence should be laid upon facilities being afforded either for a personal test or an exhibition of the powers of the engine on the level and up a steep grade. Very little heed should be taken of the owner's statements if the machine fails on this occasion, under fair and reasonable conditions, to do what is required of it.

The Vendors of Second-hand Motor Cycles.

Perusal of the foregoing remarks may, perhaps, lead the reader to suppose that vendors of second-hand motor bicycles, as a class, are prone to be dishonest, and that the inexperienced buyer is running a great risk in dealing with them. This, however, is not at all the impression which it is desired to convey. There are several firms, both in London and elsewhere, who do a large and perfectly straightforward business in this class of goods; and not only is it possible to obtain exceptional bargains from them at times, but one may always rely on receiving the expert assistance of a thoroughly competent and experienced salesman in making a selection.

The same applies to the private advertisements one sees in such profusion in the advertisement columns of the Press. Probably nine-tenths of the machines therein offered for sale are worth what is asked for them, and often more perhaps;

FIG. 167.—The "Triumph" 3½ h.-p. Motor Bicycle.

but there remains the odd tenth, and it is because of this fact that readers are warned to be as careful as they possibly can in purchasing a second-hand machine.

Purchasing a New Machine.

The fortunate individual who can afford to pay cash down for a brand new mount is relieved of a lot of worry in that he has a host of good firms' productions to choose from, and he may take it that the condition of the machine will be all that can be desired when it is delivered to him. It is important that the order should be placed as early in the year as possible, for the makers, none of them, go in for turning out large numbers of any one pattern on chance;

but work according to the run of orders, so that as long as from eight weeks to three months often elapses between the date of the order and that of delivery. Lest this statement be contradicted, the author might, perhaps, quote the

Fig. 168.—The "Norton" 4 h.-p. Motor Bicycle, with "Roc" Two-speed Gear and Free Engine Clutch. Suitable for side-car work.

experience of a personal friend. Four prominent makers, one after the other, required the order to be placed early in January, for delivery by Easter in two cases and Whitsun in the other two, of that year. This is, perhaps, an extreme case, but it is generally several weeks before one can obtain their new machine.

Having once acquired a motor bicycle, and learned how to drive and manage it, a new interest is created in the life of the possessor. No longer need he depend on the railway time-table when desiring to make a journey of any length. It is often not only as quick, but actually quicker, to go by road, and how much greater is the enjoyment of so doing— given, of course, reasonable weather and other conditions. The fact is brought home with considerable force where the journey is a cross-country one, and one, or perhaps two, changes have to be made *en route*, and the author has himself frequently scored over the railway under these and similar circumstances.

FIG. 169.—The " P. & M." 3½ h.-p. Motor Bicycle, with Chain-drive and Two-speed Gear.

Various Types and their Capabilities.

The motor cycle is essentially a pleasure vehicle, but at the same time its capabilities are such as to render it an invaluable aid to commercial travellers, doctors, road surveyors, and others whose work takes them out and about at all times of the day; and a point worth mentioning here is that, where frequent stops and re-starts have to be made, it is advisable to use a lightweight machine (for town and runabout

MANAGEMENT OF THE MOTOR CYCLE. 215

purposes) and a clutch or two-speed model or monocar where longer distances and heavier going have to be provided against.

Always remember that some day or other you will be wanting to sell your motor bicycle, so go in for as good a one as possible, and take care of it *all* the time, so that a better price can be obtained when the time comes for selling.

It would occupy far too much space to set forth even briefly the leading features of the motor cycles at present on the market, and it should be clearly understood that, in selecting for illustration and special notice those of which reproductions are hereby appended, the purpose has been to convey a true impression of the different *types* of machines, irrespective of any particular claims made on their behalf by the manufacturers. The whole book might be easily filled

FIG. 170.—The New "Premier" Motor Bicycle, with Twin Engine, having even-firing intervals. (3¾ h.-p.)

with illustrations and particulars of other models equally as deserving of notice. The "Hobart" Motor Cycles comprising the models, as illustrated on page 206-8, have much to commend them. The design, construction and finish of these machines is most excellent and the makers wellknown reputation fully upheld. The 2½ h.-p. "Handy" Hobart lightweight has been consistently successful in the leading events and at the present time holds the 100 miles Brooklands lightweight record. The lady's model, also fitted with a 2½ h.-p. engine is in great demand, and has been the means of many ladies taking up motorcycling as a pastime.

The new 3½ h.-p. twin cylinder "Hobart" machine (Fig. 163) is a most attractive looking model, and is, for a twin-cylinder, comparatively light. It is strongly made, sufficiently powerful for a side car and includes the fullest equipment a motor cyclist could possibly require. The author can personally testify to the all-round excellence of "Hobart" motor cycles, having been accorded the opportunity of fully inspecting their manufacture from start to finish, and they are machines which can be recommended with the fullest confidence.

Desirable Features of Construction.

The purchaser will doubtless be guided to a large extent in making his selection by his own personal preferences, and will eventually decide on the machine which embodies, in its general design, the largest number of points which accord with his own views; but it may, nevertheless, be of use to the less experienced buyer to have placed before him a few of the essential points which he should bear in mind when endeavouring to come to a conclusion as to which machine he will have. Briefly summarised, these may be taken as follows:—

The machine should possess:—

(1) An engine, in the design of which accessibility to every part has been studied and provided for.
(2) A soundly designed and strongly made framework, with the engine so carried as to be easily detachable, if desired.
(3) A low-riding position, with a comfortable reach and adequately designed foot-rests or, preferably, foot-*boards*.
(4) Spring forks, which absorb vibration without permitting "bouncing" of the front wheel or lateral instability.
(5) Handle-bars having an easy rake, adding to the comfort of the rider and his control over the machine.
(6) A fairly capacious tank. (This, of course, depends to a large extent upon the engine power and weight of machine.) The tank-fillers should be large in diameter, especially that of the lubricating compartment.
(7) An efficient silencer (*not* an apology for one).
(8) First-grade tyres, suitably proportioned for the work to be placed upon them.

MANAGEMENT OF THE MOTOR CYCLE. 217

FIG. 171.—The "Scott" Motor Bicycle (3¾ h.-p.) with Two-stroke Twin-cylinder Water-cooled Engine.

FIG. 172.—Balancing the "Scott" prior to starting, with Engine running.

218　THE MOTOR CYCLIST'S HANDBOOK.

(9) A belt of adequate width. If chain-drive, only the best makes of chain are any use.
(10) A complete tool outfit, stand, carrier, and number-plates (these are *not* considered accessories now-a-days by good makers.)

Fig. 173.—A Powerful Twin-cylinder Motor Bicycle—the 8 h.-p. "Chater-Lea," ("J.A.P." Engine).

(11) A decent saddle; and
(12) Good finish all round. Magneto (which should be placed in a protected position, as at the rear of the engine) and carburettor of known and well-

tried reputation. General handiness, first-class enamelling and plating, lack of fancy work, and no unnecessary complication of detail.

The purchaser should not hesitate to enquire as closely as he likes into the hidden characteristics of the engine. Many leading firms publish in their catalogues interior views of the engines and other parts of the construction; but others leave the purchaser to find out from experience the features of design and class of workmanship and material he has been supplied with; and the first time he has the engine to pieces he may find evidences of faulty design, hurried workmanship, cheap labour, or other drawbacks which had he known at first would have decided him against purchasing the machine.

The Beginner's First Ride.

It is wonderful how soon a complete novice falls into the ways of motor cycling—almost at his first ride, as a rule. He should take the machine out on a quiet road and, if possible, find an easy down grade whereon he can pedal the machine without the belt in order to get used to the position and control. This done, he can next have a try with the engine running, making sure to keep the exhaust lifter and brakes handy so as to stop immediately, if occasion arises.

The "running mount" indulged in by the majority of riders should not be attempted at first, although it is easily accomplished after a little practice. The exhaust valve must be raised and the machine pushed along the road at a fair speed. Then drop exhaust lifter, and directly the engine fires, jump into the saddle, either by means of the pedal or straight off the road, immediately afterwards setting the levers as described below. As he becomes more experienced the rider will know just how to set his levers to get going easily, and his knowledge of the machine and its ways will rapidly extend. Something will be learned every time he goes out, and it will not be long before he feels himself competent to go almost anywhere and tackle almost anything that the more seasoned and experienced motor cyclist undertakes.

Driving Considerations.

The great thing in driving a motor cycle is, of course, to humour the engine as much as possible. Keep the petrol

FIG, 174.—The "Rex" 5-6 h.-p., with "Roc" Two-speed Gear and Free Engine.

FIG. 175.—The "V.S." 7-9 h.-p. Motor Bicycle, with "V.S." Two-speed Gear and Free Engine.

consumption down by running with the throttle as far closed as circumstances permit, and the air lever, on the contrary, as wide open as possible. Petrol costs money, air does not; therefore, study your own pocket by husbanding the former at the expense of the latter.

When approaching a stiff hill get all the speed on the engine possible, and begin by having both the throttle and air levers well open. Then, as she shows signs of flagging a little, give the remaining throttle, and place your finger on the air lever, slowly closing it as becomes necessary to maintain the power of the engine, by feeding it with a richer mixture. Further signs of flagging should be met by closing the extra air still more (and perhaps entirely), and then, when that is done and something more is wanted, try slightly retarding the spark lever so as to cause the ignition to take place rather later, viz., when the piston is in such a position and the crank at such an angle as to be more favourably disposed to receive the impulse. If pedalling gear is fitted use should be made of it if the engine begins to labour, and before, *not* after signals of distress have become apparent.

Do not be afraid to try the effect of *reopening* the air lever (after shutting it off as described above), by slight degrees, as the machine nears the top of the grade; or, in any case, when it appears to be mastering its task. When it has had a good feed of rich mixture it often calls for a slightly weaker one, something it can digest better, and a wonderful spurt follows the reopening of "the air." Lose no time, on reaching the summit, in closing the throttle down to its normal position, and if the climb has severely tried the engine, it is as well to run at moderate speed for a bit. The spark lever may now be advanced, but never while the climb is in progress. Every opportunity which presents itself for cooling the engine should be taken advantage of. When running down a grade, lift the exhaust valve, open the air lever wide, and partly open the throttle. Coast as far as possible, allowing the cold gas to circulate through the engine, and if a switch is fitted, use it for the purpose of suspending the sparking operation until the engine is again required. Do not let the speed get down too low before restarting the engine.

"Misfiring" occurs when too much extra air is given, for the reason that the mixture is then too weak to be exploded with the necessary force. Also, if there is any appreciable impediment in the petrol supply or the insulation of the sparking plug is defective. If any part of the high-tension cable wire should become exposed and touch any metal object, the current will be interrupted and misfiring

Fig. 176.—An American Motor Bicycle: The "Indian" 7 h.-p.; Chain Drive and Two-speed gear.

Fig. 177.—The "F.N." 5-6 h.-p. Four-cylinder Motor Bicycle, with Bevel-gear Transmission.

set up. A sticking valve or broken valve spring may cause it, and so does the presence of dirty oil on the sparking plug or contact-breaker points. The rider cannot remain long in ignorance of the fact when his engine is even slightly misfiring. The speed falls off and the noise of the explosions becomes fitful and altogether irregular. The sparking plug is usually found to be at the seat of the mischief when misfiring occurs.

Care as to Lubrication.

The continued use of a rich mixture (too much gas, too little air) is not only uneconomical, but tends to overheat the engine, destroying lubrication and generally acting adversely towards it. A pumpful of oil injected into the engine as the hill is approached helps wonderfully, and in every condition of running the lubrication of the engine must—as was emphasized in Chapter IX—be strictly attended to. The amount of oil required varies with the size and speed of the engine. A standard $3\frac{1}{2}$ h.-p.

Fig. 178.—The " T.A.C." 7 h.-p. Four-cylinder Motor Bicycle, with Worm-drive.

engine, doing solo work with an average weight of rider and luggage, requires a full pumpful of oil about every 10 to 15 miles. More when it is quite new, when it is working under adverse conditions of road and weather, or when prolonged running in a low gear is enforced, as when passing through thick and continuous traffic, and the engine is kept going at a high speed by means of a clutch or variable speed arrangement, the cooling of the engine being curtailed at the same time by the slow movement of the machine through the atmosphere.

A better method than giving a full charge of oil every so many miles is to give half-a-pumpful twice as often, as then the lubrication is effected with greater continuity—not a surplus at one time and a shortage at another. Much depends on the size of the oil pump and the quality of the oil employed.

Engine Control Methods.

As regards which is the best method of controlling the engine on the road, the reader is recommended to cultivate the throttle control method. This tends to economy in petrol consumption, certainty in results, and without doubt produces a greater efficiency all round. Raising the exhaust-lifter, when desiring to reduce speed, is all very well, but it is hard on the exhaust valves, uneconomical, and is generally called " bad driving." Switching on and off of the electrical current provides another means of control; but it is not a good one, and the engine is subjected to shocks which it might be spared by employing the throttle control system.

Either of the last-named methods conduce to the production of what is known as " popping " in the silencer, a thing which does much towards bringing motor cycling greatly into disrepute among the general public. Gases are allowed to continue circulating through the engine, and they reach the heated silencer in an unexploded state. The high temperature in the latter does the rest. The throttle method cuts down the gas, and entirely bars its passage to the cylinder when not required, and there is practically no risk of explosions taking place in the silencer in such circumstances.

FIG. 179.—A Front View of the " T.A.C." Four-cylinder Motor Bicycle.

MANAGEMENT OF THE MOTOR CYCLE. 225

The Question of Gear Ratio.

The gear ratio of a single-geared motor cycle plays an all-important part in the working of the engine. For speed work a high gear is required, and a lower one for heavy pulling and hill-climbing work. The means whereby these opposite interests are combined in the one machine have already been described, but it remains to be said that many "fixed" gear motor cycle engines are undoubtedly over-geared. The reader may require a little guidance as to what constitutes a suitable gear ratio and how he may ascertain what his particular machine is geared at.

To ascertain this latter point a small file or other mark should be made on the engine pulley, and another similar mark placed on the belt rim of the back-wheel. Get both in the topmost position — over the centre they revolve around. Then (preferably with the help of a friend) turn the back wheel one complete revolution, and note how many revolutions the pulley has made during that time. By this simple means the gear of any belt-driven machine may be at once ascertained; the number of pulley revolutions compared with the single revolution made by the belt rim, of course, constituting the gear ratio of the machine.

FIG. 180.—Rear View of the "Arno" 3 h.-p.

For ordinary touring work, taking the hills as they come in average country, a gear of $4\frac{1}{4}$ or $4\frac{1}{2}$ to 1 will suit an 11-stone or heavier rider, with luggage in addition; but, where heavy country has to be traversed, and the load is much increased, better results will be obtained with a gear of, say, 5 to 1, while for temporary purposes even 6 to 1 may be used with advantage.

An adjustable pulley will usually provide a range of gears such as this; while, if a variable speed gear is employed, it is possible, of course, to obtain a 9 to 1 gear, if required. Riders of moderate weight in plenty are employing gears of less than 4 to 1 and getting on very well with them; but one has to be very active and a good driver unless a lot of engine knocking is to take place.

"Knocking"—What it Means.

The term "knocking," referred to in Chapter VII, describes the clanking, metallic noise sometimes heard within the

Fig. 181.—Control, etc., Fittings of the " Rex " Motor Bicycle.
(A)—Automatic Lubricator. (B)—Oil Pump. (C)—Oil Tank Filler. (D)—Petrol Tank Filler.
(E)—Petrol Injector. (F)—Petrol Gauge. (G)—Carburettor on Lever. (H)—Throttle Lever.
(I)—Front Brake. (J)—Exhaust Lifter Lever. (K)—Ignition Lever.

cylinder, and caused either by reason of the gear being too high, heavy carbon deposits in the cylinder, worn bearings, or faulty driving, with spark too far advanced, at low speeds. To correct it the extra air-opening must be reduced at once, and if the knocking is very persistent a lower gear must be employed, the ignition set back a trifle, the piston, etc., cleared of carbonised accumulations, or the bearings rebushed,

Fig. 182.—The "Scott" Motor Bicycle from above.

according to which of these causes is producing the mischief. In any case it means that oscillation is being set up in the bearings and hammering action produced—to the detriment of the engine generally.

The task of re-bushing an engine is, generally speaking, beyond the powers of most motor cyclists, principally owing to lack of the necessary tools. Care should be taken to entrust this work to competent motor mechanics only, and the charge should largely depend upon whether the owner or the repairer takes the engine down and re-assembles it.

FIG. 183.—Carburettor Handle-bar Control, " Triumph " Motor Bicycle.

Some " Don'ts " to be observed.

Summarising the foregoing remarks in a series of " Don'ts " which, even though they *do* repeat what has already been said, can hardly fail to serve a useful purpose, we would say to the reader who desires to study his own interest and that of the engine he drives—

Don't run the engine for a moment longer than is absolutely necessary on the stand before starting.

Don't attempt to start the machine under almost impossible conditions, and then grumble at the difficulty.

Don't grab at the throttle and sparking handles and alter their positions suddenly, with a jerk. The manipulation should be gradual and by small degrees, unless in the case of an emergency arising.

Don't retard the magneto on hills unless absolutely obliged (to prevent knocking), and then only slowly and by small degrees.

MANAGEMENT OF THE MOTOR CYCLE. 229

Don't forget that air is cheap and petrol is not, so throttle down and run on as weak a mixture as circumstances permit.

Don't fail to take every opportunity which presents itself for cooling the engine on down grades.

Don't switch in the magneto again while running switched off, unless there is a fair speed on the engine.

Don't control the speed by frequently raising the exhaust lifter. Learn to " drive on the throttle," and rely on that method for regulating the speed.

Don't use the exhaust cut-out (if you have one) unless well away on the open road. Never open it near restive horses or when passing through the streets of villages and towns.

Don't hustle the engine unnecessarily at any time. Forced speed does harm, and one never knows when the policeman may appear from behind the hedge.

Reasonable care only, such as anyone can give, is required, and it is generally amply repaid, as not only is the efficiency of the engine and machine as a whole upheld by careful treatment; but there is a certain indefinable pleasure in looking well after one's mount, and the fact that, after all, it is a somewhat complex piece of engineering construction should never be quite lost sight of.

What the Tool Bag should Contain.

When setting out for anything in the nature of a *long* ride the motor cyclist should take with him the following kit of tools and "spares":—

A large adjustable spanner;

A smaller-sized ditto;

The set of spanners and any other special tools supplied with the engine;

Screwdriver;

Pair of pliers (combination type); another pair (quick-grip type);

Belt-punch and knife (or small saw);

Some copper wire, high-tension cable, a few assorted bolts, split pins, nuts and washers;

Two or three spare sparking plugs, a few spare magneto parts (such as high-tension carbon holder), platinum points and contact-breaker bell-crank, insulating tape and a file for touching up platinum points;

Spare belt, a couple of belt fasteners, butt-ended inner
  tube for tyre, repair outfit for ditto, tyre levers,
  and some valve rubber ;
Complete inlet and exhaust valve for engine ;
Spare carburettor jet ;
Carbide (and perhaps a spare lamp burner).

Of course, if only an ordinary pleasure outing, covering a comparatively short distance, is intended, many of the above items may well be left behind ; but the motor cyclist of average carefulness usually carries at least the outfit listed above when going any distance, and many take nearly twice as much. One may be laughed at for carrying a "blacksmith's shop in miniature" about with him. The author was on one occasion subjected to some good-humoured bantering of this description, and shortly afterwards met the banterer-in-chief in a remote part of the country late at night and stranded for want of a simple part, which was at once produced and thus saved what would have otherwise have meant, for the erstwhile joker, a four-mile trudge pushing a heavy machine.

These remarks must not, however, be taken as implying that it is necessary when motor cycling to cart a lot of cumbersome tackle about with one. Moderation is required in this as in all things ; but an article or so too much is better, when the pinch comes, than having to suffer delay and inconvenience because of some "missing link"—perhaps not worth more than a few pence when the next town is reached—but cheap at any price when out on the lonely road.

Motor Cyclists' Clothing.

As regards suitable clothing for motor cycling. In this country, at all events, it is hardly ever safe to venture out without some sort of mackintosh outer covering. Stout boots, warm underclothing, and a suit and cap of thick material are required for ordinary weather riding ; while in winter, or for night journeys, a leather waistcoat, leggings, and a good warm neck-wrap add to one's comfort. The mackintosh overall suit should be of double texture, and the jacket double-breasted. Leather gauntlets or some other heavy class of leather gloves are essential. In wintry weather the author uses a Service "Coldweather" jacket made of

MANAGEMENT OF THE MOTOR CYCLE. 231

lined Irish freize, with wind cuffs and storm collar; leather breeches, stout leggings, and boots, with, perhaps, a leather waistcoat and sweater into the bargain; and finds this combination very efficient in keeping out the most intense cold. In the summer months holland overalls are useful, but, as before said, it is never wise to go out without mackintosh protection as well. The Burberry motor clothing has special advantages of its own.

Some Hints "In Lighter Vein."

It is unwise to keep the machine at it for just so long as it will run, without ever troubling to look into the condition of the parts from time to time. Be sure that if this negligence is indulged in, the time will come, as certain as Fate, when she will let you down out on the road, and it will be miles from anywhere, for these things never happen just outside the wide-open doors of a motor garage.

Never imagine you know *all* there is to know about motor bicycles. The designers themselves don't—in spite of their wide experience, and the author of these pages realises only too well what a lot *he* has yet to learn about the subject. Let every ride you undertake teach you something, however small. Join a club or motor cycle organisation of some sort, and go where motor cyclists "get together," and keep your ears open. You will, maybe, hear a certain amount of nonsense talked, but there will be plenty of sensible and instructive conversation also, and much of it you can turn to your own advantage in a practical way. Always know you may be stranded one day (or night) where assistance is entirely unavailable, and something has gone wrong with the machine which you cannot fathom at first. You will then have to extricate yourself from the situation off your own bat, either by triumphing over the difficulty or by hard pushing till some more favoured spot is reached.

The Man or the Machine?

How many times does it occur that motor cyclists are held up on the road for hours together, when only just a *little* more knowledge of the construction of their machines and the adjustments needed to keep them in order would have enabled them to get going again in a fraction of the time. It must always become a triumph of mind over matter in these circumstances. The machine must be made to go where the rider wants to go, and do what he wants it to do, and *not* the other way about, and when she stops without his permission there is something which has to be discovered and put right. Motor cycles don't stop for nothing or just out of pure fun ; there is always a reason for it, and as they can't tell you what that reason is themselves, you have got to discover it and take the necessary steps for its removal. It is part of the game, and a very fascinating part into the bargain. Don't get easily disheartened, but put on your considering-cap, have a smoke, and go methodically to work.

There will generally be some more or less pronounced symptom to guide you, but if not there is no cause for alarm. Don't go spending an hour trying to hunt out the cause of failure unless you either know, or have first made sure, that there *is* petrol in the tank. The engine simply won't run without spirit, but many a motor cyclist has discovered, after an hour or so of fruitless endeavour, that he has been trying to make it do so.

"Shall I——" ?

Should another motor cyclist overtake you while you yourself are travelling at the speed which best suits your purpose, don't jump to the conclusion that he is necessarily challenging you to a race ; but let him go on and be the one to run into the arms of the waiting policeman. Never look condescendingly at the pedal cyclist as you pass him struggling up the hill, while you are simply roaring up. The sparking plug may give out the next moment, and then he has the laugh of you.

Always be ready to help a brother motor cyclist in a difficulty. When you come across him attending to his machine by the roadside, ease up and call out to enquire whether you can be of any assistance. A small contribution from your toolbag may set him going again, and, remember—it may be *your* turn next.

Don't heed the witticisms of the passer-by who refers to you as "another broken-down motor cyclist," whereas, perhaps, you are only making a most simple adjustment. A certain class of pedal cyclists and others delight in doing this (and to change a sparking plug even is to be " broken-down " in their view) ; but wait until you catch them up (it won't be long), and then they wish they could change places with you after all. It is much more dignified than shouting out about their being " behind the times," and so on.

"Passenger" Motor Cycling.

Having become sufficiently expert in the management of a motor cycle, the rider will probably yearn for some means of sharing his enjoyment with others. It seems rather selfish to be always prating to others about the delights of motor cycling, and the average man begins, as a rule, to feel that he would like to be able at times to offer a ride to his friends or relations, who otherwise may be quite debarred from anything of the kind.

FIG. 184.—A Montgomery Rigid Side Car.

Side Cars.

This may involve the purchase of another and more powerful motor cycle, but not necessarily so, and the cheapest and handiest method of carrying the passenger idea into effect is to purchase a side car. This can be attached and detached at will, so that either solo or passenger riding may be indulged in as fancy dictates. The author has had something like 30,000 miles of motor cycling with a side car, and finds the companionship of a passenger delightful. It is highly necessary to employ a machine of ample power and possessing a two-speed gear to secure the best all-round results; but a great amount of " fun " can be derived from a single-geared motor cycle and side car, provided, of course, that not less than 3½ h.-p. is available.

In his view it is by far the better plan to attach the side car to the *left*-hand side of the machine, as then in overtaking other vehicles the driver and not the passenger gets first view of the road ahead. Opponents of this view

FIG. 184A.—A Montgomery Castor-wheel Side Car.

assert that as the majority of motor cyclists accustom themselves to mounting from the left-hand side of the bicycle the side car ought to be connected up on the right, so as not to preclude a continuance of the practice. They also claim that the right-hand side is better for fast riding and taking sharp corners at speed. No one worth his salt, however, need make any difficulty about mounting from the right instead of the left-hand side. It is not as though he has any balancing to do.

Side Car Types.

There are three main types of side car—the rigid, flexible, and castor wheel In the first-named the wheel is held in

FIG. 185.—"Scott" Two-stroke Motor Bicycle and Rigid Side Car.

rigid alignment ; the second has flexible connections, consisting of link-work to hold it up to the bicycle frame ; and, in the last-named, the side car wheel is attached to a ball-bearing steering head, and adapted to move freely and automatically in the same direction as the front wheel of the motor bicycle. The 30,000 miles above-mentioned has included the use of all three types, as manufactured by the well-known firm of Montgomery & Co., Coventry, who specialise in this class

FIG. 186.—The " Rex " Sidette—a handsome Passenger Motor Cycle.

of work and produce a first-class article, and the opinion arrived at as a result of this is, that for all-round convenience, freedom from slipping, and simplicity, the rigid side car is the best. It is, of course, the cheapest to purchase. If properly aligned with the bicycle the wear on the tyres is but little increased, but it cannot be too urgently impressed upon prospective users of this form of machine that where it is intended to employ a powerful engine and go in for real touring or general road work the driving tyre of the bicycle should be of larger section than usual. It is worth while going to the additional expense of a 2½-in. tyred rear wheel as compared with the more usual 2¼-in., as this permits of a stouter tyre being used and one better calculated to withstand the extra strain thrown upon it. The only drawback to the practice of employing different sized tyres being that interchangeability is sacrificed. The side car may not be a mechanically correct form of attachment, but it is an uncommonly handy and pleasant one to use, nevertheless.

Other Passenger Types.

Tricars or forecars are not now enjoying popularity with the motor cycling public. They were formerly considered the type *par excellence*, but that day is now passed and gone. Their popularity may possibly be revived, but they would have to be made both lighter and less expensive to allow of it.

The "Sociable" type of three-wheeled passenger motor cycle has much to commend it. It is the ideal "small car" in very miniature, and possesses all the principal attributes of the motor bicycle, with, of course, added comfort and protection from the weather. It is classed by the taxation authorities as a tricycle, and thus (so long as it does not weigh more than a certain load)— see next chapter—it escapes the higher grade of taxation.

FIG. 186A.—Method of Aligning a Motor Bicycle and Side Car.

The Auto-Carrier (A.C.) "Sociable," illustrated on the next page, is a good example of the type. It has an air-cooled 5-6 h.-p. engine and epicyclic two-speed gear, chain-drive, free engine (multiple disc-plate), clutch and tiller steering. Fitted with cape hood and wind screen, it

Fig. 187.—The "Auto-Carrier" Tandem Tricar.

Fig. 188.—The A.C. "Sociable."

provides a very taking and handy form of passenger motor cycle.

The Auto-Carrier firm also manufactures a tricar model, of which an illustration is appended. The same class of engine and means of transmission is fitted in this case.

Of late there has sprung into being a type of motor tricycle or runabout on three wheels, in the design of which a single steering wheel is placed in front, and the double wheels at the rear, while a comfortable single- or double-seated well enclosed body is fitted. The best example of this type is that of Messrs. A. W. Wall, Ltd., of the "Roc" Motor Works, Birmingham (see page 240.) It is, possibly, a fact that this class of machine is more stable in grease and when taking corners than when the opposite arrangement of wheels is employed, and it is quite likely that this has guided certain manufacturers in introducing the new type. Then there is the recently introduced "Morgan-Runabout," which can be obtained either with a twin or single-cylinder air-cooled engine. A very "classy" little car at a reasonable figure.

Passenger motor cycling has a charm of its own, and those who can afford to do so may well decide to keep a medium weight bicycle for their own individual use and another machine for passenger carrying.

The Cost of Motor Cycling.

It is generally supposed—by those who have not tried it—that motor cycling is an expensive pastime, and, inasmuch as the terms "costly" and "expensive" are very elastic ones, they can be made to mean almost anything. It is quite possible to obtain a very large measure of enjoyment from motor cycling in return for a comparatively small outlay. The purchase of the machine is the most serious item, new machines of recognised make costing from about £35 to close upon £70 ; but a fair average figure is £48. It depends largely upon the make and horse-power, and whether the machine be a single-geared, clutch, or variable-geared one. Accessories, licensing, and other fees, help to mount up the initial cost ; but, once this has been got over, the owner may, if he go carefully and intelligently to work, run the machine very cheaply as compared with the great benefits he will derive from its use.

The thing is to keep the machine as much as possible out

240   THE MOTOR CYCLIST'S HANDBOOK.

Fig. 189.—The "Wall" Motor Tricycle, with comfortable Side-entrance Body, Two-cylinder Engine and Two-speed Gear.

Fig. 190.—The "Morgan Runabout" Engine fitted in front of car

of the repairer's hands, but not to neglect consulting a competent repairer, when the necessity arises, for work which cannot be done properly at home. Petrol (at the time of writing) costs 1s. 1d. per gallon (in and around London) to 1s. 4d. (out on the country roads), and something between these two limits in most country towns. The best lubricating oils can be had for 1s. 6d. to 1s. 8d. per sealed quart tin, and less *pro rata*, if bought in larger quantities. These two commodities, and especially the former, need replenishing more frequently than anything else, and constitute a leading item in the running expenses. From 80 to about 100 or 120 miles can be obtained from a gallon of petrol on average roads; but a quart of engine oil goes very much further.

As before stated, good second-hand motor bicycles can be purchased for quite moderate sums, £20 securing a very fair magneto model, while for £30 (in the middle of the "off" season) some rare bargains can be obtained. The author commenced his motor cycling career some years ago on a machine costing, second-hand, £16, and it proved an unqualified success. In many cases motor bicycles have been purchased for as little as £8, and even then have proved satisfactory bargains. When the figure reaches such a low level as that, however, too much must not be looked for. The machine will necessarily be of old pattern, with accumulator ignition and some obsolete fittings, and may require a fair amount of work done upon it before it can be classed as in really satisfactory "going" order. If the purchaser is possessed of a workshop with a fair equipment of tools, he may easily be able to turn a poorly-conditioned second-hand motor bicycle, purchased at a low figure, into a very serviceable mount by his own energy and skill, combined with a moderate cash outlay. Passenger motor cycling naturally entails greater expense than otherwise would be incurred.

CHAPTER XIII.

Accessories and Equipment.

The experienced motor cyclist knows full well how necessary it is, if complete satisfaction is to be obtained from his machine, to be careful in the selection of the accessories he intends to use with it. As in the case of the machines themselves, there are different grades of quality in the various fitments made and sold for attachment to motor cycles, and the purchaser will do well to study the design of these and investigate the more important points connected with their manufacture.

There is a tendency among some motor cyclists to disregard the importance of this part of our subject and to cut down as much as they possibly can the amount spent on the accessories and equipment of their machines. This, to say the least of it, is a "penny wise and pound foolish" policy, for unless the articles are thoroughly well-made and of good materials, they not only fail to give satisfaction while they last, but the "lasting" itself is only quite a brief business.

Motor Cycle Tyres.

First of all, the owner of a motor cycle should make very sure that the *tyres* fitted to his mount are good ones, and of adequate proportions for the work to be done; and if he takes the following short table as his guide he cannot go far wrong:—

    For motor bicycles of $1\frac{1}{2}$ h.-p. to 2 h.-p., $1\frac{3}{4}$-in. tyres.

    For motor bicycles over 2 h.-p., up to 3 h.-p., 2-in. tyres.

    For motor bicycles of $3\frac{1}{2}$ h.-p. to 4 h.-p., $2\frac{1}{4}$-in. tyres.

    For motor bicycles of 5 h.-p. to 8 h.-p., $2\frac{1}{2}$-in. tyres.

    For the rear wheels of tricars and special machines for carrying two passengers (apart from bicycle and side car combinations), a "Voiturette" tyre (about 3-in.) will give the best results.

ACCESSORIES AND EQUIPMENT.

In order to prevent, as far as possible, the danger of side-slipping, motor cycle tyres are now-a-days made with rubber-studs or other projections on the treads, and in some cases

Fig. 191.—The "Dunlop" Motor Cycle Tyre, with Studded Tread.

Fig. 192.—Section of "Kempshall" Motor Cycle Tyre Outer Cover.

the non-slipping qualities of these are so small as to be almost negligible. Others, however, are perfectly efficient, and, speaking from his own experience, the author can testify to the good qualities of the Dunlop tyre—a pair of which, used on a heavy 5–7 h.-p. motor bicycle, hauling for the greater part of the time a side car and passenger—lasted for nearly 7,000 miles before having to be retreaded. Palmer Cord, Continental, Kempshall tyres are other excellent productions, all of which motor cyclists can safely rely upon.

Fig. 193. The "Kempshall" Tyre.

Considerable popularity is enjoyed by the detachable type of inner tube for motor cycle use. This may be either open or butt-ended; but, in any case, its removal from the wheel when the rider requires either to repair a puncture or to replace the tube by another, is greatly facilitated, as once the outer cover has been released from one side of the rim, the tube may be taken right away in a few seconds and another put in its place.

The butt-ended tube is, perhaps, the easier to fix in place and inflate, as in its case there is no joint to trouble about, whereas in the open-ended detachable tube, unless the jointure between the two ends is carefully made, so as to be absolutely air-tight, it becomes impossible to inflate the tube at all. It is, however, a comparatively easy job to secure this airtight

Fig. 193A.—" Shamrock Excelsior " Motor Cycle Tyre.

joint between the two ends. It is advisable, when entering the ends of the tube in the butt-ended type to sprinkle them well with French chalk, so as to prevent friction and the probability of rubbing through of the tube.

The use of steel studs in the tyres of motor cycles has gone somewhat out of favour of late years, although one very good tyre has rubber diagonal bars with steel studs in between. Rubber studs are very effective as skid preventers, and they last a reasonable time; they hold the road well in very loose dust and on frozen roads, whereas steel-studded treads do neither. As a general rule, motor cycle tyres are

Fig. 193B.—" Peter-Union " Non-skid Pneumatic Tyre.

Fig. 194.—The "Dunlop" Butt-ended inner Tube, with Retaining Flap which fits over Valve.

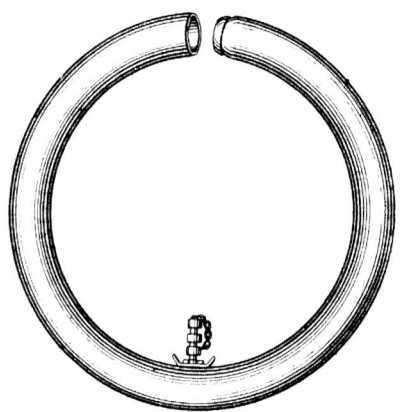

Fig. 195.—The "Rich" Detachable Inner Tube (open-ended).

Fig 195A.—How the Air-tight Joint is made in the "Rich" Inner Tube.

made with beaded edges instead of being wired on. It is advisable to keep them pumped up hard while riding and always to carry a *really* good tyre-repairing outfit and suitably proportioned levers for removing the outer cover to repair or exchange a tube. A decent-sized and well-made pump is also a fixed necessity.

By far the greater proportion of the wear falls upon the rear (driving) wheel tyre, this having to withstand greater weight and added friction; the power of the engine in driving the machine being, of course, transmitted to the road through the rear wheel. It is a good plan to change the tyres over when the non-skid tread on the back one is worn down; this tyre being placed on the front wheel and that of the latter going on to the rear wheel, this, of course, being rendered impossible in the case of unequal sizes of tyres. When both are quite smooth—but not seriously cut or otherwise damaged—a new tread can be vulcanised on at a cost of from 14s. 6d. to one guinea per tyre, and in this way considerable further service may be obtained.

If matters are allowed to go too far, however, and the inner fabric of the cover is cut about much, it may be found impossible to carry out the vulcanising process with success; and, in any case, the inner portion of the cover would have to be specially repaired, thus adding to the cost of the work. The strength of the walls of the tyre is an important consideration, for the addition of a heavy vulcanised tread increases the strain thrown upon them.

If good tyres are necessary on a motor bicycle so is a good belt, in order that the power developed by the engine may be transmitted with efficiency, and as large a percentage of it as possible utilised in driving the machine (in accordance with the output at various speeds), for otherwise there cannot possibly be satisfactory working.

Belts and Belt Fasteners.

As remarked in a previous chapter, the belt must possess strength, flexibility, and a sure grip of the pulleys; and if only one of these attributes is missing the belt, as a whole, will fail to come up to what is required of it. Rubber and canvas belts are very popular, being clean to handle and capable of more minute adjustment in respect of length than are most leather belts. The latter, however, as before said, last longer and seldom break; they are very strong, but need carefully attending to; occasional lubrication to keep them pliable, and somewhat frequent scraping of the effective surfaces on which, in course of working, grit and grease accumulate, being required.

The two leather belts specially referred to in a previous chapter will both be found highly suitable for their purpose, and both have the advantage of being easily shortened when required.

In selecting a belt-fastener, make sure that it is easily detachable, for many so-called "detachable" fasteners require a lot of patience and pulling about to get them apart. Motor cyclists are not perhaps the most patient of all people; they being accustomed to move along quickly, and to be kept hanging about trying to get the belt fastener adrift or reassembled, perhaps in the rain or intense cold, suggests profanity with not a few.

In the author's opinion the best type of belt fastener is that which, in addition to being detachable, allows of variation in its length by using longer or shorter links or hooks as required, and the manner in which this is effected may be gathered from the sketches appearing in Chapter VIII. The fastener, to be satisfactory, must be strongly made and care should be taken to use the proper size of fastener as made for attachment to a given width of belt.

Tyres and belts may be better classed as "equipment" than as "accessories"; but they have been purposely included in the present chapter as coming within the range of renewable parts in the purchase of which the motor cyclist will have to exercise his own judgment.

The Lamp Question.

A very essential accessory on a motor cycle, and one which should *always* be of good quality, is the head-lamp. It is quite possible now-a-days to buy a large, showy-looking lamp for quite a moderate sum, but it is false economy to do so. The lamp should, above all, be substantially made, possess a first-class lens, and have riveted instead of brazed or soldered joints.

It is not always the largest and heaviest lamps which give the greatest amount of light, neither should the intending purchaser allow himself to be carried away too far by the

Fig. 196.—The New " Dunhill " Acetylene Headlight for Motor Cycles.

Fig. 197.—Sectional Drawing of Separate Generator Type Acetylene Headlight.

(A)—Burner.　(B)—Lens Mirror.　(C)—Front Lens.　(D)—Rubber Gas Tubing.　(E)—Water Compartment of Generator.　(F)—Carbide Container of Generator.　(G)—Needle Valve Adjuster.　(H)—Water Filler Cap.　(I)—Gas Pipe.

mere outward shape and appearance of the lamp. Space prohibits anything in the nature of even a brief treatise on the subject of light-giving in connection with motor cycle lamps ; but it may be said that a really good head-light will throw a beam of as much as 600 ft. in front of the machine, and nothing is more strictly necessary, where much night riding on main or other roads in the country has to be done, than that a powerful lamp should be used.

Most motor cycle lamps are of the acetylene gas burning type, and most are provided with separate generators, so that a powerful light may be obtained, and the necessity of recharging made as infrequent as possible, without concentrating all the weight of the lamp in one unit. Smaller lamps having the generator in one with them and of rather less capacity are made, these being known as of the "self-contained" type, and they have the advantage of clipping all in one piece on to the lamp bracket.

In some few cases the makers have designed separate generator lamps, in which the generator is attached to the same bracket as the lamp itself. In this case the clip is fixed, as a rule, to the handle-bar stem, as seen in the accompanying illustration, which shows the "Service P. & H." headlight—a very powerful light-giver substantially made, and, indeed, a high-class production all through.

The latest Dunhill lamp is also illustrated. This is rather smaller than the other, but the light it gives is nevertheless exceedingly strong and penetrating, and the lamp is scientifically designed and well made. Other well-known motor cycle lamps are the Lucas ("King of the Road"), "F.R.S." and "Seabrook Solar," and the reader will be perfectly safe in investing in either.

It is highly necessary to employ a very strong clip for attaching the lamp and generator to the machine. Makers are fully alive to this fact *now*, but a few years ago it was a common thing for motor cyclists to have their lamps smashed, or at least seriously knocked about, as a result of the clip breaking and the lamp being dashed to the ground.

Satisfactory results can only be obtained, even from the very best lamp made, so long as the user is prepared to keep the generator clean internally, the burner free from getting sooted up, and only a really good brand of carbide should be used.

Electric headlights are sometimes used on motor cycles, and the author has experienced much satisfaction from employing the "Glare," made by Messrs. Greenwood & Co., of Halifax. This lamp is provided with a hinge, so that it can be tilted up to read the directions on sign-posts, and the

Fig. 197A.—The "Service" P. & H. Acetylene Headlight.,

Fig. 198.—The "Glare" Electric Headlight.

current is supplied by an accumulator neatly enclosed in a metal case, lined with india-rubber, and provided with clips for attachment to the frame or handle-bar of the machine. These lamps are very useful indeed for inspection purposes, as with them there is no fear of an explosion should there be an overflow of petrol. The lamp question is an important one with the motor cyclist, and he is urged not to grudge the money required to buy a really good article.

ACCESSORIES AND EQUIPMENT. 251

Horns, Sirens, and Exhaust Whistles.

We may next devote a little attention to the subject of appliances designed for creating audible warning of the motor cyclist's approach. These include horns (or hooters, as some prefer to call them), exhaust whistles, and sirens. The first-named are most largely used, but the other two, and especially the whistle, enjoy a fairly considerable vogue.

Again, it is false economy to buy any but a strongly and well-made horn, and special attention should be devoted by the purchaser to the clip attachment. This, in very many cases, is quite inadequate for its purpose, and the rider is subjected to the annoyance of its breaking, while a common fault is that the horn either revolves around the handle-bar or goes dancing about upon the latter, setting up an irritating chatter, and gradually wearing away the plating. A horn is of very little use unless:

(1) It creates a loud sonorous sound;

(2) Has a fair-sized rubber bulb, and well-made reed ; and

(3) A strong, properly fitting clip.

Of late there has been a tendency to introduce what are known as tri-note or "fanfare" horns, having three separate horns attached to one stem and bulb. In the author's view this type is not to be recommended. The noise it makes is an especially irritating one to other road-users, and it is

Fig. 200.—The author obtained better results by forming a baffle inside pipe, thus deflecting gases to whistle.

Fig. 199.—The "Dunhill" Exhaust Whistle.

necessarily a more complicated piece of construction than the single type of horn. A good, substantial, well-made single- or double-twist horn, leaves nothing to be desired.

Exhaust whistles are very effective as road clearers. They perhaps work better with a twin engine, owing to the more continuous exhaust; but they also do very well on a single-cylinder engine, and command attention where the more usual " hooter " fails to do so. Sirens, worked off the tyres, also produce a very powerful sound, but the exhaust whistle (so-called, of course, because it is operated by the exhaust gases) is more certain in action, more durable, and does not even minutely affect the speed of the machine. In fact, it rather assists it, as it acts, in a measure, like a cut-out when in use.

Motor Cycle Saddles.

The saddle is an all-important adjunct of the motor cycle, and stress has already been laid, in the chapter on " Springing," on the necessity for using one which is properly designed and made.

The saddle should be springy, without being what may perhaps best be described as " bouncing." The rider desires to be insulated, as far as possible, from vibration, but without being nearly bounced out of his seat. His comfort depends very largely indeed upon the quality and character of the saddle, and only the best-known makes should appeal to him.

The Brooks B-104 motor cycle saddle, with padded top and compound coiled springs, as illustrated, on page 179, is a very comfortable one indeed, and much of the succecss and high reputation rightly credited to it is due to the fact that the springs are proportioned to the particular rider's weight. This fact should be borne in mind when purchasing a saddle of this kind, or when the bicycle one has selected is fitted with it. The makers always desire to know the rider's weight, and they will then supply a saddle having springs suitable thereto.

Another excellent saddle is the Middlemore D.L. pattern (see page 179) mounted on twin-tension spiral springs, and having a comfortably padded top. A good saddle costs as much as from 23s. to 30s., but it is cheaper then than an inferior one at little more than half the money.

ACCESSORIES AND EQUIPMENT. 253

Luggage Carrier and Stand.

The purchaser of a motor cycle should carefully inspect the stand and carrier supplied with it. These must be strongly made, and the stand (by means of which the back wheel is held off the ground) should have some easy means of fastening when not in use. In some cases the stands are

FIG. 201.—Luggage Carrier and Stand for Motor Cycles.

made to spring upwards, and automatically lock themselves in position as the wheel is dropped to the ground, and if properly designed this is a great convenience.

It is common practice to make the carrier of tubular material, thus adding strength to the construction and reducing the chances of the bags or other packages carried upon them getting chafed. The practice, at an earlier stage, was to make the stand and carrier in one, and every time the rider wished to perch his machine up he had to remove the tool-bag, etc., before he could do so; and, further, as the carrier was mounted on the rear wheel spindle, when he wanted to take the wheel out the stand became inoperative. Nowadays, however, the two are made separately from one another, and, moreover, the legs of the stand are hinged on to a lug on the chain stays, so that in taking out the back wheel the stand may be used for supporting the machine.

Stands are made either with separately controlled legs or with a cross-piece connecting them and, everything considered, the latter plan is perhaps the better one, except where a side car is used, for then only one leg—the outer one—is required. The makers usually supply the all-in-one-piece type of stand, it being more simple to make, and very easily attached. Front-wheel stands are not often seen, but they come in very useful for tyre repairing, wheel adjusting or removing, and so on. A tendency to extend the use of these stands is manifesting itself, and in time, no doubt, they will come to be regarded as a standard fitment.

Tool Bags and Equipment.

The average motor cyclist, when setting out for a long ride, takes a spare inner tube and a spare belt with him. Sometimes—indeed, very often—he ties them up and hangs them on the machine, wherever he can find a place, by means of string or a strap. Much better is it to invest in one of the neat, combined tube and belt cases now on the market. These are strongly made of leather, and of circular shape. The tube is coiled up in a separate central compartment, while the belt space lies outside of this, as seen in the illustration. Both articles are kept dry, free from getting chafed, and always ready for immediate use.

The tool bag (or bags) should also be capacious and *anything* but flimsily made. They have to withstand a lot of hard wear, and are preferably fitted with metal linings to prevent holes being worn through them by contact with the tools. The latter, or the heavier ones among them, should be wrapped up in pieces of rag, and matters should be so organised that delicate spares, such as sparking plugs,

ACCESSORIES AND EQUIPMENT. 255

carburettor and magneto parts (if carried), small nuts and washers, and other small sundries be kept apart in a bag by themselves. Spare valves should also be wrapped up and kept from contact with heavier items, and so should insulating tape, high-tension wire, and, in fact, anything likely to get easily damaged or broken.

Some idea has already been afforded of what the tool kit should comprise, and it is, of course, quite impossible to enlarge on that part of the subject in any degree of completeness.

Fig. 202.—Combined Tube and Belt Case (Priory Accessories Company, Coventry.)

Fig. 203.—Metal-lined Tool Bag.

Fig. 204.—Terry's Turbine Spanner.

Special spanners and other appliances are to be had by the hundred from the leading accessory dealers and others, some being excellent, but others—well, not so good.

The Terry spanners, shown on the next page, have been found extremely useful by the author, who makes a rule of always carrying them. They are strong without being bulky (a great point in their favour), and the adjustments permitted by the turbine spanner are very minutely graded.

A good and complete tyre repair outfit is compulsory, and the rider should never neglect to carry one with him. Never be deluded into buying cheap and nasty sparking plugs. Their use is fatal to good results. The same applies to belt fasteners, and, indeed, to every part—large and small—of the machine and its appurtenances.

Fig. 205.—A useful case of Spanners (made by Terry and Sons, Redditch)

Fig. 206.—How the Belt Punch works.

Fig. 207.—The " A.M.A.C." Belt Punch.

It is possible nowadays to obtain tube patches (Surridge's "Holdtite") which do not necessarily require solution to fix them (petrol being sufficient for the purpose). These are particularly useful to the tourist.

Speedometers.

The use of a speed indicating and mileage recording device on a motor cycle greatly adds, not only to the convenience, but also to the pleasure of the rider. It is extremely useful and interesting to know at what speed you are running, and not only this, but it becomes almost imperative to be able to correctly judge the speed when travelling through ten-mile limits, and otherwise where the police are known to be actively on the track of motorists. But if one is going to invest in a speedometer, and rely upon it as a means of gauging the speed of his machine, he must be very 'ware of the cheap inaccurate type of instrument which, so far from helping him to clear keep of a trap, will more likely than not lead him into one by showing a lower speed than that at which he is in reality travelling.

FIG. 208.—The "Triumph" Magneto Shield.

The "Jones" Speedometer.

The "Jones" speedometer has been found by the author to be extremely accurate, and it is known that in very many cases where motorists have been summoned for exceeding the speed limit the testimony of this instrument has been accepted by the Bench as evidence in favour of the defendant. It is simple in construction and splendidly made. The dial and mechanism casing clips on to the handle-bar, and an enclosed flexible cable, carrying at its lower end a toothed bevelled gearwheel, which engages with a similarly toothed ring, is secured to the spokes of the front wheel, as shown ; the cable and pinion being supported in position by a suitable bracket bolting on to the front-wheel spindle. The rotary movement of the cable actuates the mechanism of the indicator, and the indication of the speed and recording of the mileage is very accurately and minutely performed.

Fig. 210.—The "Jones" Speedometer (Front Wheel Fittings).

Fig. 209.—The "Jones" Speedometer Dial on Handle-bar.

Fig. 211.—The "Veeder" Mileage Recorder, attached to Front Wheel Spindle

The instrument is made in three forms for motor cycle use—
i.e. (1) indicating up to 60 m.p.h., and showing the season's mileage ; (2) indicating to 60 m.p.h., showing season's and also the daily mileage ; and (3) speed to 60 m.p.h., season or total mileage in tenths and miles, and also the daily mileage. This last-named model is fitted with maximum hand and instantaneous reset mechanism (Fig. 209).

A cheaper but thoroughly reliable instrument for recording only the distance travelled by day and by year (without speed indicating) is the " Veeder," made for attaching to the front-wheel spindle.

Both of the above-referred-to appliances are supplied by Messrs. Markt & Co., Ltd., of City Road, London, E.C.

Miscellaneous Accessories.

The carrying of a watch on the handle-bar tends to increase the pleasure, is also a useful practice, and special carriers are now sold together with a cheap but good pattern watch, all ready to go straight on to the handle-bar.

Of " special " motor cycle accessories there are no end. Many of them can well be done without, except, perhaps, by the very fastidious. Remember that everything you add to the machine increases the load the engine has to propel, and it is astonishing how these accessories help to total up in the aggregate. Good and well-made fitments, of not too bulky or ponderous proportions, should be selected, and, lastly, don't have anything to do with anything smacking of the " freak " description. There is no room for these on your motor bicycle.

CHAPTER XIV.

THE LAW IN RELATION TO MOTOR CYCLING.

THE use of a motor vehicle on the public roads is permitted by law under certain conditions which must be strictly adhered to, and the motor cyclist is just as much bound to observe these conditions as is the owner of a 60 h.-p. motorcar.

Driving Licence.

He can purchase as many motor cycles as he likes, but, strictly speaking, he cannot even push one of them, if completely equipped for riding, along a public thoroughfare unless it carries identification numbers, while before it is possible (in a legal sense) to drive the machine a single yard a driving licence must be obtained. The intending purchaser of a motor cycle should apply to the County Council of his own or some other county for (1) a driving licence, and (2) registration numbers. These will each cost 5s., and before either is granted he has to fill up a form giving particulars of the machine, and his own name and address, say whether he has held a licence previously, and give various other particulars, all of which are, however, very quickly answered. If the applicant is under fourteen years of age, he will have to bide his time until he has reached that age.

Number Plates.

Having secured the driving licence and identification numbers, the latter must be painted on two separate plates—one for attachment to the front of the machine, and the other to the rear. The letters must be a distinct white on a black ground, each figure or letter measuring $1\frac{3}{4}$ ins. high by $1\frac{1}{4}$ ins. wide by 5-16ths in. thick everywhere. The distance between the top and bottom edges of the plate, and those of the lettering must be $\frac{1}{4}$ in., while $\frac{1}{2}$ in. of margin must be left at each side.

The space between the letters and figures must be ⅜ in. The letter "I" and the number "1" need only be 5-16ths-in. wide,

Inland Revenue Licence.

In addition to the fees already mentioned it is necessary to take out an Inland Revenue, or "carriage" licence. This costs £1, and can be obtained at any post office. It requires annual renewal (during January) and lapses on December 31st in each year. Motor cyclists applying for carriage licences any time during the last quarter of the year receive an abatement of half the amount charged for the full year. The drivng licence is also renewable annually.

The charges apply equally to a small-powered lightweight motor cycle and to a high-powered passenger machine. Side cars (attached to motor cycles), tricars, and other three-wheeled motor vehicles weighing not more than 3 cwts., unloaded, at present come within the same scale ; attempts have been made in certain districts to levy a charge on side cars, but so far without success, but if a trailer or other type of passenger or luggage carrying attachment on two wheels is used, a fee of £2 2s. becomes payable.

Regulations Governing the Sale of Motor Cycles.

If the owner of a motor cycle sells his machine he will, if he desires to keep his original numbers for use on a new one, have to apply for their cancellation and re-issue to himself, and the fee for this is 5s. If, however, he sells the machine, and the new owner takes the numbers over with it, the latter can apply to the County Council for transference of the numbers to himself, and for this he will be required to pay 1s.

It is very necessary that *both* the old and the new owners should notify the authorities, and failure on the part of either to do so may result in a visit from a police officer with, possibly, more or less unpleasant consequences to follow.

Illumination of Number Plates.

One or other of the number plates must be illuminated at night, and the easiest way out of this is, of course, to place the front plate where the headlight can shed a part of its rays upon it. No need then to illuminate the rear number plate. The law does not require you to do so,

Neither are you obliged to carry a number plate on the back of a side car, but if a trailer is used it must carry a plate. The best plan is to employ a number plate for the front wheel which is painted on both sides, and secured to the mudguard in a longitudinal position, so that the light from the lamp may play on both sides of it.

As regards a rear light, although there is no obligation to do so, it is well to carry one, and it should, of course, show a red warning to overtaking traffic. A very 'cute idea has recently come on to the market in the shape of a combined rear identification plate and red rear light. It is called the "Self-lighting" plate and is sold by the Priory Accessories Company, of Coventry, at a very low figure, including both the plate and lettering.

FIG. 212.—The "Self-Lighting" rear Number Plate.

The accompanying illustration shows the arrangement. The registration in this case was issued by the Coventry District Council.

Speed Regulations.

A maximum speed of 20 m.p.h. is permitted on the highways, and anyone found to be exceeding this may be stopped, his name and address taken, and a summons for "exceeding the limit" issued. He is liable to be fined for riding his machine while not having his licence upon him, and must be prepared to exhibit the licence whenever required to do so by a police officer.

Most towns (and very many villages) have a ten-mile speed limit—a few have a five-mile limit—and any excess of this may lead to an appearance in court. Other offences include riding to the common danger, or in a manner dangerous to the public, and cases have been known in which motorists have been convicted and fined under this heading when their speed was below that of the prescribed local limit, the policeman having given it in evidence that, in his opinion, the number of people in the street, or other circumstances, made it dangerous to proceed even at that moderate speed.

As an instance of this, a friend of the author's was summoned and fined at a Petty Sessions for having "driven a motor cycle in a manner dangerous, etc.," through the main street of a little village, and the police-sergeant in charge of the case admitted, under cross-examination, that the speed did not exceed 7 to 8 m.p.h., the rider pulling up in one-and-half lengths of the machine when called upon to do so.

Should the rider be stopped for exceeding the speed limit alone he must either be warned by the police, at the time, of intention to prosecute, or such notice must reach him within three months of that date. If it does not, and he is subsequently summoned, he should urge the lack of notice in his defence.*

Should he be carrying a speedometer, and be keeping down the speed by its aid to less than that alleged by the policemen, he should direct the latter's attention to the fact, and should take steps to have the instrument tested by the makers; and then, if summoned, call their representative to give testimony to the fact of its accuracy. It seldom happens that the speedometer (if a good one, and properly fitted) tells an untruth.

Brake and other Regulations.

A motor cycle is required by law to carry two separately controlled brakes. A clear light in the direction of travel must be shown from one hour after sunset to one hour before sunrise. Audible warning of approach must be given whenever necessary, the rider must stop his engine in response to the upheld hand of anyone in charge of a restive horse, and if the machine is left unattended on the roadway steps must be taken to prevent its being started by others.

The Storage of Petrol.

Petrol may be stored up to a maximum quantity of 60 [gallons without a licence. In London 48 gallons only is allowed. It must be kept in metal cans and stored apart from a dwelling-house. The rules in this respect

---

* It does not do to rely on this point as it is frequently disallowed by country Benches.

are only applied with stringency where larger quantities of petrol are stocked. The keeping of a sealed can or two immediately adjacent to, or actually within, the house would hardly be objected to, but the motor cyclist who is wise generally keeps the spirit well away from all chance of its getting accidentally ignited.

A Final Word.

In conclusion, the author sincerely trusts that what has been written in the present volume may prove useful to its readers, and should any of them at any time desire to correspond with him on the subject of motor cycles and motor cycling he will be happy indeed to reply to any letters addressed as follows:

"PHŒNIX," c.o. The Editor,

The Model Engineer and Electrician,

26 to 29, Poppin's Court, Fleet Street,

London, E.C.

A Racing Motor Cyclist—A. V. Deacock on 5 h.p. "Wanderer" at Brooklands Track.

"THE MODEL ENGINEER"

Edited by PERCIVAL MARSHALL, A.I.Mech.E.

This is published every Thursday, price 2d., and is a splendid practical journal of mechanics and electricity. A column of most interesting "Motor Cycle Notes" is contributed every week by "Phœnix," the author of this handbook, and there are frequent articles on petrol motors, coils, batteries, and workshop matters of service to motor cyclists. The journal gives thoroughly sound information by expert writers, but is not too technical for the amateur to easily understand. If you want to buy or sell a Motor Cycle or accessory try an advertisement in our motor cycle columns. "The Model Engineer" is read in workshops all over the world, and is popular everywhere. Get this week's issue from your newsagent: :: :: :: you will like it. :: :: ::

We give Personal Instruction
--- in ---
Motor Cycle Repairs.

Personal instruction in the use of the lathe and in soldering, brazing, coil winding, motor repairing, and all kinds of mechanical and electrical work may be had in "The Model Engineer" Laboratory. You can build your own motor cycle engine, or make or repair any parts or fittings for your machine under personal instruction, at your own time. The workshop is equipped with first-class lathes and machine tools, and the instruction is adapted for the beginner as well as for the advanced worker. Tests of dynamos, motors, coils, batteries, etc., can be made and defects explained and remedied. Send for illustrated prospectus, or call and see us.

"THE MODEL ENGINEER"
26-29, POPPIN'S COURT, FLEET STREET, LONDON, E.C.

INDEX.

	PAGE
A.C. Sociable Tricar	237
A.C. Tandem Tricar	238
Accessories and Equipment, Motor Cycle	242
Accumulator Ignition, Wiring and Connections	86
Accumulators	86

Accumulators—
  Construction and Handling of 113
  Recharging 86, 113
  Voltage of................... 113
Acetylene Headlights 249
Adjustable Pulleys 124
Adjustment of—
  Automatically-operated Inlet Valves 188
  Belts 120
  Petrol Level in Carburettor 82, 194
  Timing Gears 14
  Trembler Coil............ 114
  Trembler Coil for Twin-cylinder Motor........... 115
Advantages of Free Engine Clutches 129
Air—
  Carburettor ; Permanent Supply to 66
  Carburettor ; Supplementary Supply to 67
  Cooling 45, 160
  Spring System, the A.S.L. 168, 177
Alignment—
  of Belt Pulleys 122
  of Side Cars 236
Amac Belt Punch............. 256
Amac Carburettor, The........ 72–74
Angle of Pulley Faces, Importance of Accuracy in 118
Apparatus, Ignition 84
Apparatus, Ignition, On Second-hand Machines, Testing the 210
Armature—
  Action of the.............89–93
  Direction of Rotation......89, 96
  Short-circuiting, Consequences of............... 90
  Winding of the........... 89–93

	PAGE
Armstrong-Triplex Three-speed Gear	155
Arno Engine, Features of the	50, 194
Arno Motor-Cycles	209

Auto-Carriers—
  Sociable Tricar (see A.-C.)
  Tandem Tricar (see A.-C.)
Automatic—
  Carburettors 78
  Inlet Valves 11, 19
  Inlet Valves, Methods of Adjusting 188
  Inlet Valves, Testing........ 190
  Lubrication 162
Auto-Varia Pulley, The Lloyd.... 132

"BACKFIRE," Meaning and Consequences of a 103
Back-pressure 56
Bags (Tool)..................... 254
Ball-bearing Engines............ 51
Bat, Spring-frame Motor Bicycle 174
Batteries—
  Dry.....................84, 112
  Primary 85
  Secondary 86
Bearings (Engine) Main Shaft 51
Bearings (Engine) Rebushing 22
Belt—
  Fasteners 120, 247
  Pulleys, Alignment of...... 122
  Punches 256
  Slip 118
  Stretching of the 120
  Tension, Maintaining the 140, 143
  Tensioning Device, The Wanderer 126
Belts 116–126, 246
Belts—
  Adjustment and care of .. 120, 126
  Carrying 254
  Round Twisted 118
Bevel-gear Drive, F.N. System of 123
Bicycle Parts, Care of the 202, 211
" Blowing-back " in Carburettor 189
Bosch Magneto Ignition 92
Bosch Magneto for Twin-cylinder Engines 92, 96, 98

Are You a ✌ ✌ Motor Cyclist?

IF SO, you cannot afford to be without—

GAMAGE'S new Motor Accessory List

The most comprehensive ever published.

GRATIS AND POST FREE.

A.W. GAMAGE Ltd, HOLBORN. BENETFINK & Co Ltd, CHEAPSIDE. LONDON.

	PAGE
Bosch Sparking plugs	111

Brakes—
    Legal Requirements *re* .. 201, 263
    Motor Cycle, Types of 201
Break (of Platinum points) 197
Brooks Saddles, Compound Spring
    Type 179, 252
Brown & Barlow (" B. & B. ")
    Carburettors 70, 72
Butt-ended Inner Tubes (for
    Tyres) 243

CABLE High-tension 84, 112
   Carbon Deposits in Cylinder 191
Carburettor—
    Adjustments 66, 80, 194
    Control 67
    Function of the 63
    Jet, Effect of Changing the.. 75
    Position of the 31
    Spray Type, Action of the 65-69
    Successful Working, Importance of 67
    Surface Type, Action of the.. 63
    The Amac 72-74
      Brown & Barlow (" B and
        B ") 70-72
      J.A.P.—Automatic 78
      Longuemare 80
    Tuning up the 80, 194
Care of the Ignition Appliances .. 108
Carriage (or Inland Revenue)
    Licence, The 261
Cells—
    Primary (*see* Dry Batteries).
    Primary, Voltage of........ 112
    Secondary (*see* Accumulators).
    Secondary, Voltage of 113
Chain Drive—
    (or Transmission) 122
    The Indian 123
    The " P. & M. " 150
    The Scott 122
Chamber, Distribution or Timing
    Gear 52
Change-speed Gears and Clutches 138
Chater-Lea Motor Bicycle, The .. 218
Chater-Lea Spring Forks 169
Clair Silencer, The 56
Clothing, Motor-Cyclists' 230
Clutches—
    Free Engine, combined with
      Two-speed Gears 138
    Free Engine, Types and advantages of 127-137
Coils, Induction—
    Accumulator Ignition 86
    English and French, Marks on 88
    Non-Trembler Type .. 87, 114
    Trembler, Adjusting........ 114

	PAGE

Coils, Induction—
    Trembler Type 87, 114
Combustion of Gases in Cylinder.. 105
Combustion, Rate of, Effect of
    Compression upon........ 62
Compression—
    Loss of 60, 182
    Ratio of 61
    Restoring the 182, 190
    Stroke (Four-stroke system) 7, 60
    Testing the 209
Condenser, Function of the 95
Conductors, Electrical 83, 112
Connecting Rod, Design of the .. 47
Connecting Rods for Twin-cylinder
    Engines 49
Connections (and Wiring)—
    Accumulator Ignition 86
    Bosch (Magneto) Ignition .. 92
Consumption—
    Electrical Current 108, 114
    Petrol 75
Contact Breaker—
    Function of the 87
    Types of 87, 94, 112
Continental Motor Cycle Tyres .. 243
Control—
    (Carburettor), Handlebar Type 67
    (Carburettor), "Tank" System 68
    Engine.................... 224
Cooling the Engine 97, 221
Cost—
    (First) Question of when
      purchasing Machine 206
    of Motor Cycling 239
    of Petrol.................. 241
Crank-Case—
    Construction of the 51
    Hot, Explanation of 60
    Oil-retaining Joints for 51
Cubic Capacity of Cylinder, Calculating 209
Current, Electrical—
    Collection and Distribution of 96
    Consumption of 108, 114
    Generating 83-85, 88
Cycle—
    The Four-stroke 7-10
    The Two-stroke 20-25
Cylinder—
    Arrangement in Twin-cylinder
      Engines 31
    Carbonised Deposits in, Removing 191
    Combustion of Gases in the.. 105
    Jointings, Compression Tight 190
    Removing and Replacing the 191
Cylinders—
    Cubic Capacity of, Calculating 209
    Design and Construction of.. 45

BOSCH MAGNETO

on your machine means a perfect ignition service.

The wonderful precision which marks the construction of every Bosch Magneto guarantees its absolute reliability. This means, of course, that you secure permanent satisfaction at minimum cost during the lifetime of the machine.

Bosch Magnetos are made in types suitable for all makes of motor cycles.

THE BOSCH MAGNETO Co., Ltd.,
40 & 42, Newman St., Oxford St., London, W.

Telegrams—"Bomag, London." Telephone—Gerrard 430 (five lines).

	PAGE
Cylinders—	
Effects of wear upon	184
Mountings	55
Re-boring	184

DELIVERY of Motor Cycles, delay in 212
Deposits, Carbon, Removal of.... 191
Detachable Belt Fasteners... 120, 247
Detachable Inner Tubes (for Tyres) 243–5
Diagnosing—
    Carburettor Faults 194
    Engine Faults 181
    Ignition Faults............. 196
Difficulty in Starting Engine..... 195
Distortion of the Magnetic Field.. 90
Distribution (or Timing) Gear 13, 34, 52
Distribution (or Timing) Chamber 52
" Dont's " for the Motor Cyclist.. 228
Double Trembler (for twin engines) Adjusting 115
Douglas Engine (twin-horizontal type) 35
Douglas Motor Bicycle, The..... 211
Drip, Lubrication 162
Drive—
    Belt 116–120
    Chain..................... 122
    F.N. Shaft and Bevel-gear... 123
    Magneto (types of) 52, 104
    T.A.C. Shaft and Worm Gear 124
Driving Licence, Obtaining the .. 260
Driving, Motor Cycle, Hints on... 219
Druid Spring Forks........ 167, 169
Dry Batteries............... 84, 112
Dry Batteries, Voltage of 112
Dunhill—
    Acetylene Head-light, The .. 248
    Exhaust Whistle 251
Dunlop—
    Belt 118
    Butt-ended Inner Tubes..... 245
    Tyres 243–5

ECONOMICAL Driving, Hints on 219, 221
Electric—
    Current, Generation of 83, 85, 88
    Headlight, The " Glare " ... 250
    Headlights 250
    Insulators 83
    Spark Ignition, Advantages of 82
    Spark, Production of the 83
Electrical—
    Apparatus, Faults Connected with 196
    Matters, Motor Cyclists and.. 82

	PAGE
Engine—	
Bearings, Rebushing........	228
Control Methods	224
Horse-Power, Calculating....	208
Maintaining the Power of the	181
Overhauling and Tuning Up the	180
Power, Avoiding Excessive..	207
The " Arno " 50,	194
" Douglas "	35
" F.N." (four-cylinder) ..	42
" J.A.P."..............	38
" Norton "	17
" Peugeot "	18
" Premier "............	39
" Rex " 26,	34
" Scott " (two-stroke) ..	20
" T.A.C." (four-cylinder)	44
" Triumph "............	15
" Wanderer "	41
Working Principle of the	7

Engines—
    Ball-bearing 51
    Equal Power in Cylinders of, Obtaining 12
    Four-cylinder 39, 42
    Four-stroke System 7–11
    Horse-Power of, Calculating. 208
    Twin-cylinder, Working System in 30
    Two-stroke System....... 20–29
    Two-stroke, Petrol Consumption of 20, 27
    " V " Type.............. 30–40
    Valveless Type............. 20
Epicyclic Gearing 147
Equipment, Motor Cycle 242
Evolution of Ignition Methods... 82
Excessive Engine Power, Need for avoiding 207
Exhaust—
    Box (or Silencer)........ 55–58
    Lifter Mechanism 188
    Pipe, Design of the 55
    Valves 10, 52
    Valves, Springs for 17, 19, 53, 188
    Stroke, The (Four-cycle) 7
    Whistles 251
Expanding Pulley Type, Variable Gears 140
Expansion of Gases in Cylinder... 105
Expenditure, Considerations of, when Purchasing 204
Explosion Stroke, The (Four-cycle) 7

FAULTS—
    Carburettor, Diagnosing.. 81, 194
    Engine, Diagnosing......... 181
    Ignition, Diagnosing........ 196

"Hints and Tips for Motor Cyclists."

¶ SAVES TIME, TROUBLE AND TEMPER, YET COSTS 1/-

¶ THE SECOND EDITION OF THIS EXTREMELY USEFUL BOOK, CAREFULLY COMPILED AND BROUGHT RIGHT UP TO DATE, IS NOW READY. ITS CONVENIENT SIZE, EASY ACCESSIBILITY, AND COMPREHENSIVE INFORMATION, RENDERS IT INDISPENSABLE TO THE MOTOR CYCLIST.

PRICE 1/- net, or by post 1/2,
from all Booksellers.

WHEN ON TOUR

CONSULT THE

"Motor Cycle" Route Book.

¶ IT IS A BOOK SPECIALLY COMPILED FOR USERS OF THE HIGHWAY IN THE UNITED KINGDOM.

¶ MOTOR CYCLISTS WILL FIND ITS INFORMATION INVALUABLE. THE BEST ROUTES ARE GIVEN, SMOOTHEST SURFACES STUDIED, THE MOST INTERESTING PATHS CHOSEN. BE SURE AND SECURE A COPY BEFORE STARTING ON TOUR.

PRICE, 1/6 net, or by post 1/9,
from all Booksellers.

**ILIFFE & SONS, Ltd.,
20, Tudor St., London,**
E.C.

	PAGE
Features of Motor Cycle Construction, Desirable	216
Features of Spring Fork Design	172
Fees, Licensing	260
First-cost, Question of, when Purchasing Machine	206
First Ride, The Beginner's	219
Fixed Ignition	90, 100
Flooding the Carburettor	68
Flywheels, Design and Weight of	50

F.N.—
    Four-Cylinder Engine 42
    Motor Bicycle.............. 222
    System of Bevel-gear Drive. 123
Force, Magnetic Lines of......... 89
Forks, Spring—
    Desirable Features in....... 172
    Principles of Design in 165
    Types of 166–176
Formula, R.A.C., for Calculating Horse-Power 208
Forward Belt Fastener, The 121
Four-cylinder Engines 39
Four-speed Gear, The Osborne .. 153
Four-stroke Cycle, The 7–10
Frames—Spring
    The Bat 173, 175
    N.S.U. 173, 176
    Wanderer 173
Free-Engine Clutches... 127, 134–137
Free-Engine Clutches—
    Advantages of 129
    Combined with Change-speed Gearing 138
    Manipulation of 132, 137

GAP, Correct between Valve and Tappet 187
Gap, Sparking Plug Points 84, 110, 197
Gas (Petrol), Production of...... 66
Gear—
    Drive, Magneto 52, 104
    Ratios 125, 225
    The Armstrong-Triplex Three-Speed 155
    Gradua Infinitely Variable 139
    Indian Two-speed .. 150–153
    Mabon Infinitely Variable 142
    Millennium Fit-all....... 154
    Osborne Four-speed 153
    P. & M. Two-speed 149
    Roc Two-speed 145–149
    T.A.C. Three-speed 140, 157
    V.S. Two-speed 143
Gearing—
    and Transmission 116
    Considerations of 225
Gears—
    Change-speed and Clutches.. 138

	PAGE

Gears—
    Change-speed, Manipulation of 158
    Change-speed, Necessity (or otherwise) of .. 140, 155, 158
    Valve Timing 13, 34, 52
Generating Electric Current 83, 85, 88
"Glare" Electric Headlight, The 250
Gradua Variable Speed Gear, The 139
Grinding in Valves 60, 185
Gudgeon Pins, Methods of Securing 47–9
"Gumming-up" of the Piston, 160, 203

HANDLEBAR—
    Control (Carburettor) 67
    Magneto Cut-out 91
Headlights—
    Acetylene 247
    Electric 250
Hellesen Dry Battery 85
High-powered Motor Cycles, Some disadvantages of 207
High Tension—
    Cable and Connections (Ignition) 112
    Electric Current 83, 85, 88
    Magneto Ignition (Bosch) .. 92
Hill-Climbing, Hints on 221
Hints—
    For the Beginner 219
    On Driving a Motor Cycle .. 219
    On Purchasing a New Machine 204, 212
    On Purchasing a Second-hand Machine................ 204–8
    "In Lighter Vein" 231
Hobart Motor Cycles 206-8, 215
"Holdtite" Tyre Repair Patches 256
Horns (or Hooters) for Motor Cycles 251
Horse-power—
    Method of Calculating 208
    Maintenance of 181
Hot Crank-case, Explanation of.. 60
Hub Type Free Engine Clutches 134, 137
Humber Motor Cycle, Roc 2-speed Gear applied to 148
Humouring the Engine 219

IDENTIFICATION (or Number) Plates 260
Identification (or Number) Plates, Illumination of 261
Ignition—
    Accumulator 86
    Apparatus, Faults connected with the 196
    Appliances, Care and Adjustment of the 108-115
    Coils 86

Everything for the Motor Cyclist.

The Motor Bike Back-rest affords users "Arm-chair" comfort. Price 7/6 each.

MOTOR-
CYCLING
COMFORT
AND
PLEASURE
IS ASSURED
IF YOU
USE AND
INSIST
UPON
USING

"CHEMICO" SPECIALITIES

It would be absurd for us to attempt to enumerate, much less detail, our numerous ease, pleasure, and comfort affording specialities in so little space, but what we have done is to illustrate a few which *no* motor-cyclist should be without.

The "**CHEMICO**" **NOISELESS OUTFIT** was designed by ourselves to meet your wants. The cover is made of leather and contains a plentiful supply of all materials to overcome all repairs. Chalk and Solution are packed in unbreakable receptacles. Price 2/6 each. The "**CHEMICO**" **CARBIDE CARRIER**, 2/- complete with ½ lb. tin "Chemico" Carbide, is indispensable to the Motor Cyclist. At 1/6 per quart, or 2/6 per ½ gallon, "**Chemico**" **Motor Bike Oil** is the best. "**Chemico**" **Carbide**, obtainable of all Agents and Garages, is the best and cheapest, at 7d. per lb. Write for particulars of **Back-Rest**, also any other information you may require.

The "Chemico" Booklet, M.C.H., post free upon request.

THE COUNTY CHEMICAL Co., Ltd.,
Box M.C.H., BIRMINGHAM.

Ignition—
  Double-pole (Lodge System) 105
  Dry Battery 84
  Fixed, or Non-variable 100
  Magneto System of 88
  Methods, Evolution of 82
  Permanent Setting of the .. 101
  Production of Electric Spark
    for..................... 83
  Systems Compared 107
  Theory of 105
  Timing of the 97-100, 200
Indian—
  Chain Transmission System 123
  Motor Bicycle, The 222
  Spring Forks 168
  Two-speed Gear and Free
    Engine 150
Infinitely-Variable Speed Gears—
  The Mabon 142
  The Zenith-Gradua 139-141
Inland Revenue Licence, The .. 261
Inlet (or Suction) Stroke, The
  (Four-cycle) 7
Inlet Valves—
  Automatic 11, 19, 54
  Automatic Adjusting 188
  Mechanically-operated 11, 52
Inner Tubes, Detachable Type (for
  Tyres).................... 243
Insulators, Electric 83
Internal Combustion Engine, The 7
Iridium, Contact-Breaker Points.. 112

JACKS (or stands), Motor Cycle
  Rear Wheel 253
J.A.P.—
  Automatic Carburettor...... 78
  Automatic Lubricator....... 162
  Engine with Overhead Valves 38
  Gudgeon Pin Fastening ... 47, 49
Jet—
  Amac, Construction of the .. 75
  "B and B" Carburettor, Removing from 71
  Size of, for Different Purposes 72
Joints—
  Compression Tight ..60, 110, 190
  Oil Retaining............51, 192
Jones' Speedometers for Motor
  Cycles 257

KEMPSHALL Tyres 243
"King-of-the-Road" Acetylene Headlight 249
"Knocking"—
  in the Engine, Meaning of
    the Term........ 62, 103, 226
  Predisposing Causes of.... 226-8
  Remedies for 226

LADY'S Motor Cycle: The
  Hobart................... 215
Lamps—
  Acetylene 247
  Electric 250
Law Relating to the Motor Cycle.. 260
Legal—
  Limit of Speed 262
  Requirements as to Brakes 201,263
  Requirements as to Number
    Plates 260
  Requirements as to Storing
    Petrol 263
Lettering on Number Plates
  (Regulations for) 260
Lever, Timing, Function of the.. 94
Licences—
  Driving 260
  Exhibition of, when Demanded 262
  Inland Revenue (or Carriage) 261
Lightweight Motor Bicycles.. 206, 214
Limit, Speed in Towns, etc..... 262
Lines of Force, Magnetic........ 89
Lloyd Auto-Varia Free Engine
  Device 132
L.M.C. Motor Bicycle, with Auto-
  Varia Pulley 133
Lodge—
  Double-Pole Ignition, The... 105
  Sparking Plug 110
Longuemare Carburettor, The.... 79
Loss of Compression, Causes of 60, 182
Loss of Engine Power, Causes of.. 81
Low-Tension—
  Electric Current, Generating 83, 88
  Magnetos 107
Lubricant, Character of the...... 160
Lubricating—
  Danger of Under 161
  Effect of Over 161, 164, 223
  Hand Force Pumps......... 160
  Oil, Cost of.............. 241
  Oil, Selection of Brand...... 160
Lubrication—
  Automatic 162
  Drip System of............ 162
  General Hints on 163, 223
  Inadequate, Symptoms of ... 163
  of Motor Cycle Engines..... 159
Lucas, Acetylene Headlight...... 249
Luggage-Carriers, Motor Cycle ... 253

MABON—
  Free Engine Clutch (Multiple
    Disc type)............... 129
  Variable Speed Gear 142
Machine as a Whole, The 204
Magnetic Field—
  Distortion of the 90

PROTECT YOURSELF.

THE BEST SAFEGUARD FOR MOTOR CYCLISTS.

Combined Rear Red Light and Number :: :: Plate. :: ::

Fitted by leading Motor Cycle Manufacturers and used by all well-known riders.

Complete, with numbers as illustrated - **3/6,** post free
Plain, without letters - - - - **2/6,** ,,

THE LIGHT THAT WILL NOT FAIL.

THOMSON-BENNETT MAGNETOS.

All British; guaranteed for two years.

Type OS_1, Single Cylinder, **£4 12s. 6d.**

Type OS_2, Two Cylinder, **£5 12s. 6d.**

All other Accessories, Lamps, Plugs, Horns, Belts, Carburettors, Belt Fasteners, Speedometers, etc.

WE SPECIALIZE IN IGNITION FITTINGS.

THE PRIORY ACCESSORIES Co.,
Priory Mill, COVENTRY.

Magnetic Field—
  Lines of Force 89
Magneto—
  High-tension Ignition System 88
  Ignition, Starting with .. 103, 136
  Power required for Driving the 91
  Setting 101, 104
  Wiring and Connections 92
Magnetos—
  Actuating Mechanism (Magneto Drive) 52, 93, 104
  Bosch High-Tension 92
Mainshaft (Engine) Bearings..... 51
Maintaining Power of Engine.... 181
Mechanically-Operated Valves (M.O.V.) 11, 53
M.E.P. in Four-stroke and Two-stroke Engines compared 29
Middlemore Saddles, Twin-Tension Spring Type 179, 252
Millennium Fit-All Two-speed Gear 154
Miscellaneous Accessories........ 259
Misfiring 112, 114, 221-3
Montgomery Side Cars 233, 236
Morgan-Runabout, The 239
Moto-Reve Motor Bicycle—
  Single-cylinder 204
  Twin-cylinder 205
Motor—
  Four-stroke, Working Principle................... 7–11
  Two-stroke, Working Principle................. 20–29
Motor Bicycle—
  The Arno 209, 225 and frontispiece
  Bat Spring Frame 174
  Chater-Lea, J.A.P....... 218
  Douglas................ 211
  F.N. (Four cylinder).... 222
  Hobart 206-8, 215
  Indian 222
  L.M.C. 133
  Moto-Reve 204
  New Hudson 138
  Norton 213
  " P. & M." 214
  Premier 215
  Rex 220, 236
  Scott (Two-stroke) 217, 227, 235
  "T.A.C." (4-cylinder) .. 223
  Triumph 212
  "V.S." 220
  Zenith-Gradua 141
Motor Cycle—
  Advantages and Capabilities of the 214
  Law 260-4
  New, Purchase of 204, 212

Motor Cycles—
  Second-hand, Purchase of 212, 241
  Types and first cost 206, 241
Motor Cycling, The cost of 239
Mounting a Motor Cycle, Styles of 219
Multiple Disc Plate Clutches 129, 134-7

N. A.B. Spring Seat Pillar...... 178
  Needle-Valve—
  Carburettor 65, 68, 74
  Adjusting 195
New Hudson Motor Bicycle, Method of Starting 138
New Machines, Purchasing 212
Non-Slipping (or "Non-Skid") Tyre Covers 243
Non-Trembler (or plain) Ignition Coils 87-114
Norton—
  Engine 17, 54
  Motor Bicycle, The 213
N.S.U. Spring Frame, The 175
Number Plates 260
Number Plates—
  Illumination of 261
  "Self-Lighting," The 262

OFFENCES Against Motor Law 262
  Oil, Engine Lubricating—
  Character of 160
  Cost of 241
  Pump 159, 163
Oil-retaining Joints 51, 192
Oil Shortage, Symptoms of 163
Osborne Four-speed Gear, The .. 153
Over-Lubricating Engine, Consequences of......... 161, 164
Overhauling and Tuning-up the Engine 180
Overhead Valves.......... 12, 34, 38
Overheated Engine—
  Remedy for 163
  Symptoms of 163
Outfit, Some Remarks on 230

PALMER Cord Tyres 243
  Paraffin Injections, Cylinder 55, 191, 203
Passenger Motor Cycling .. 233-8, 241
Path of the Magnetic Lines (Magneto Ignition) 89
Permanent Setting of the Ignition 101
Peter-Union Tyres 244
Petrol—
  Consumption 75
  Cost of 241
  Level in Jet of Carburettor, Altering 81, 194
  Storage of 263

THE WALL
"All-Weather" Tricycle
(WITH SIDE ENTRANCE BODY).

THE TRIUMPH OF THE OLYMPIA SHOW.

PRICE - - 75 GUINEAS.

Provides all the luxury of car riding at a Motor Bicycle's expense of upkeep.

ENTIRELY FREE FROM VIBRATION.
SAFE ON GREASY ROADS.
EASY TO DRIVE.

Most suitable for Doctors and Professional Men requiring to ride in comfort and to preserve an appearance of cleanliness.

Write for Lists to the Sole Manufacturers and Patentees:—

A. W. WALL, Ltd.,
Roc Motor Works,
HAYMILLS, BIRMINGHAM.

Makers of the famous Roc (Live Axle Patent) Two-Speed Gear as fitted by the leading firms under Roc License and supplied in a form to convert existing Fixed-Gear Machines.

Petrol—
   Strainers 195
Peugeot—
   Engine 18
   Gudgeon Pin Fastening, New
     Method 49
Piston—
   Construction and Design of .. 46
   "Gumming-up" of the.. 160, 203
   Rex, The 27
Piston Rings—
   Fit of 182
   How to Remove without
     Breaking 183
   Number and Type 46
   Slots, Arranging the 184
Piston (Scott) with Deflector 25
"P.-L." Accumulators 113
Phelon & Moore (P. & M.)—
   Motor Bicycle 214
   Two-speed Gear 149
Plain (or Non-Trembler) Coils 87, 114
Plate Clutches 127-137
Plates (Identification or Number) 260
Platinum—
   Economising 114
   Points (Contact-breaker)
              94, 98, 104, 112
   Points (Ignition Coil) 114
Plugs, Sparking 84, 110
Points, Sparking Plug, Adjustment of 110
Pole-pieces for Twin-cylinder
   Engines (Magneto Ignition) 92
Power—
   Engine, Diagnosing Causes
     of Lost 81
   Engine, Maintaining........ 181
   Horse (h.-p.), Calculating the 208
   Required for Driving Magneto 91
Powers Engine, Range and Selection of 206
Pre-Ignition 103
"Premier" Engine—
   Twin-cylinder Even Firing,
     The 37-41
   Single-cylinder Dual Exhaust 59
"Premier" Motor Bicycle 215
Pressure, Mean Effective (M.E.P.)
   in Two-stroke Engines 29
Primary Cells (see Dry Batteries).
Principle of Working—
   in Bosch Magneto 93
   in Four-stroke Engine 7-10
   in Four-stroke Twin-cylinder
     Engines 32-7
   in Two-stroke Engines 20-9
Priory Accessories Co.—
   Belt and Tube Case 255
   Self-Lighting Number Plate.. 262

Pulley—
   Auto-Varia, The 132
   Correct Angle, Method of
     Testing 118
   Expanding Type Variable
     Gears 140
   Wanderer Under-Geared, The 126
Pulleys—
   Adjustable Type 124
   Alignment of 122
Pump (Engine Lubricating).. 159, 163
Punch (Belt-punch), How to Use
   the 256
Purchasing—
   A New Motor Cycle, Hints
     on 204, 212
   A Second-hand Motor Cycle,
     Hints on 209-12

QUESTION of First Cost and
   Type (when Purchasing
   Motor Cycles)............ 206

R. A.C. Formula (Calculating
   h.-p.).................... 208
Ratio—
   of Compression 61
   of Gearing 125, 225
Rear Light on Motor Cycles 261
Rear Springing of Motor Cycles 173-9
Re-boring Cylinders 184
Re-bushing Engine Bearings 228
Re-charging Accumulators....... 113
Recorder, Mileage (and Speedometer), The Jones 257
Registration of Motor Cycles 260
Regulations—
   Governing Brakes 263
   Governing Exhibition of Driving Licences 262
   Governing Issue of Driving
     Licences 260
   Governing Number (or identification) Plates........ 260, 262
   Governing Number (or Identification) Plates, Illumination of 261
   Petrol, Storage of........... 263
   Sale of Motor Cycles 261
   Speed of Motor Cycles....... 262
   Use of Motor Cycles........ 260
Release Valve, Crank-case 52
Removing—
   Automatic Inlet Valves..... 190
   Carbon Deposits 191
   Carburettor Needle Valve... 195
   Carburettor Jet ("B. & B.") 71
   Cylinder and Fittings........ 191
   Engine 194
   Engine Pulley 200

1911 MODEL.

Fast,

Light,

Efficient.

This is the 3½-4 h.p. Single Cylinder

PEUGEOT

Motor Cycle Engine with M.O.I.V.

And all the Latest-Improvements.

NOTE THE ADVANTAGES IT OFFERS.

No induction pipe is necessary; the carburettor fits directly on to the inlet port union.

With or without the assembling unit illustrated, it can be fitted into most current types of motor bicycle frames.

The silencer is fitted with aluminium ends for lightness, and a ratchet "cut out" on the left side for efficiency.

The internal details are improved, and are fine examples of Peugeot workmanship, which is world-renowned.

Bore, 84 m/m.; Stroke, 90 m/m.; Cubical capacity, 499 c/m.; Height over all, 19 ins.; Width of Crank Case, 9 ins.; Diameter of Flywheels, 8 ins.; Belt Line, with 1 in. Belt—2½ ins.; Weight, 54 lbs.

Illustrated Price List on application to

J. TAYLOR, 318, Percy Road, BIRMINGHAM.
Sole Wholesale Agent.

	PAGE
Removing—	
Mechanically-Operated Valve Springs	186
Piston Rings	183
Repairers, Motor Cycle	241
Re-treading Motor Cycle Tyre Covers	246
Rex—	
Cantilever Seat, The	179
Hub-Type, Free Engine Clutch	134
Motor Bicycle, The	220, 236
Spring Forks	171
Twin-cylinder V Type Engine	34
Two-stroke Engine, The	26
Rich Butt-ended Detachable Tyre Tube, The	245
Rings, Piston, Removing	183
Roc Spring Forks, The	170
Roc Two-Speed Gear	145
Runabout Motor Tricycle, The Morgan	239

SADDLE—
Brooks' Compound Spring, The 179, 252
Middlemore's D.-L., The 179, 252
Saddles, Motor Cycle.... 165, 179, 252
Scott—
Motor Bicycle...... 217, 227, 235
System of Transmission 122
Two-stroke Engine, The .. 20, 53
Seabrook-Solar Acetylene Headlight, The 249
Seat Pillars, Spring 177
Second-hand Motor Cycles .. 181, 209
Second-hand Motor Cycles, Improving 241
Selecting a Motor Bicycle, Hints on 204–8
Self-Lighting Number Plate, The 262
Service—
Belt, The................. 118
P. & H. Acetylene Headlight, The 249
Setting, Magneto.......... 101, 104
Setting, Magneto, for Twin-cylinder Engines 104
Shaft Transmission 123
Shamrock—
Excelsior Tyres 244
Gloria Belts 118
Short-Circuiting—
Armature 90, 199
Sparking Plug 198
Side Car Alignment, Method of Obtaining Correct 236
Side Cars.................... 233–6
Side Cars and the Question of Engine Power............ 208

	PAGE
"Sidette," The Rex	236
Side-Slip	243
Silencer—	
"Popping" in the	224
The "Clair"	56, 58
Silencers, Design of	56
Simplex Belt Fastener, The	121
Slipping Belt	118
Spanners, Motor Cycle	255
Spare Parts (Engine), What to Carry	229
Spark—	
Points, Adjustment of	110
Production of the Electric (Ignition)	83, 93
Timing of the Electric (Ignition)	94, 100
Sparking Plugs, Types (and Construction) of	84, 110
Speed—	
Engine, Loss of	188
Legal Restrictions as to	262
Limits in Towns, Observing	262
Speedometers—	
Advantages of Using	257, 263
The Jones	257
Sphinx Sparking Plugs	111
Splash Lubrication, Principle of..	159
Spray Carburetters	65, 81
Spring Forks	165
Spring Forks—	
The "A.S.L."	168
Bat	174
Chater Lea	169
Druid	167
Indian	168
Rex	171
Roc	170
"T.A.C."	172
Triumph	168
Truffault	166
Wanderer	176
Spring Frames, Bat, N.S.U., and Wanderer, The	173-6
Spring Seat Pillars	177
Springing Devices—	
Adaptable	176
A.S.L., The	177
N.A.B. Seat Pillar, The	178
Rex Cantilever Seat Pillar, The	177, 179
Xl-All	176
on Motor Cycles	165
Springs—	
Automatic Inlet Valves	19
Compression (and Tension) Compared	166
Mechanically Operated Valve, Strength of	17, 53
Stands (or Jacks), Motor Cycle Rear Wheel	253

To MOTOR CYCLISTS

WE shall be happy to mail you, post free, our large illustrated catalogue of **Everything Electrical** which is full of most interesting lines, of interest to motor cycle engineers and riders.

Send now for a copy.

IMPORTANT!

The Volex self-generating Motor Cycle Electric Lamp is the perfect luxury in lamps for motor cycles.
INEXHAUSTIBLE, always ready.
Send for particulars —you should know all about it.

Note Carefully the Address—

Universal Electric Supply Co.,

BROOK STREET,
C.-on-M.,
MANCHESTER.

Contractors to H.M. Government.

Established 20 Years.

VOLT and AMMETERS.

All readings, large variety, thoroughly reliable

Prices from **2/11** each.

The "PENETRA."
The strongest, most efficient and reliable electric lamp for motor cycles; can be used to work from our "Volex" self-generator or from accumulator. Price complete, with 4-volt metal filament bulb, **10/-**

Best English-made
SPARKLING PLUGS.
The Imperial - Price **3/9**
The Arden - ,, **2/3**
Equally suitable for magneto or coil ignition.

The "HYDRANAMO."
Coupled water motor and dynamo, charges accumulators effectively from the cellar tap on pressures of 40 lbs. and over.
Price, **£3**

ACCUMULATORS (Ignition).

Most reliable and lasting, withstand vibration, ideal for motor cycle use.

4 volt. 4 amps, **6/6**
4 ,, 12 ,, **9/-**
4 ,, 20 ,, **10/6**
Large range.
See our Catalogue, post free.

The VOLTALITE.

Self-generating magneto electric cycle lamp. Brilliant light at all speeds, highly recommended by the technical Press and users. Price, **£1 1s.**
Full particulars on application
Similar type (Volex) made for motor cycles Send for particulars.

	PAGE
Stanley Belt Fastener	121
Starting (Engine)—	
by Handle	136
by Means of Free Engine Clutch	138, 144, 217
Difficulty in	195
Methods of	203
Steel-studded Tyre Covers	244
Strainers, Petrol	195
Stretching of the Belt	120
Suction (or Inlet) Stroke, The (Four-cycle)	7
Surface Carburettor, Action of the	63
Surridges " Holdtite " Tyre Repair Patches	256
Switch Magneto Cut-out	91
Synchronising Sparking Moments in Twin-Motors	92, 104
Syrens, Motor Cycle	251

T.

A.C.—	
Four-cylinder Engine	44
Motor Bicycle	223
Shaft and Worm Drive	124
Spring Forks	172
"Tank Control" (of carburettor).	68
Tension Springs, Relative Disadvantages of	166
Terminals—	
Accumulator	86
Ignition Coil	87
Magneto (and Cable)	96
Terry—	
Belt Fastener, The	121
Spanners	256
Spanners, Turbine Pattern	255
Testing—	
Accumulator Current	196
Angle of Pulley Faces	118
Automatic Inlet Valve Springs	190
Compression	209
Compression Joints	110, 190
High Tension Cable	199
Ignition Adjustments	199, 201
Magneto Setting	197
Second-hand Machines, Condition of	209, 211
Sparking Plugs, Condition of	199
Theory of Ignition, The	105
Three-cylinder Engines, Scarcity of	39
Three-speed Gear—	
The Armstrong Triplex	155
The "T.A.C."	157
Timing—	
Gears, Engine	13, 34, 52
Lever, Function of the	94
of the Spark while riding	98
The Ignition (Magneto System)	100, 199

	PAGE
Tool-bags	254
Tool-bags, what they should contain	229
Tools, Valve Grinding	185
Touring, Suitable Gear Ratios for	225
Transmission—	
and Gearing	116
Belt	116, 120
Chain	122
Shaft and Gear	123
Trembler Coil, Adjustments	87, 114
Triumph—	
Engine, Standard 3½ h.-p.	15
Hub Type Free Engine Clutch	136
Motor Bicycle, The	212
Spring Forks	168, 171
Truffault Suspension Spring Forks, The	166
Tubes (Inner) Detachable Types of	243, 245
Tuning-up the—	
Carburettor	194
Engine	181
Turbine Spanner, Terry's Patent	255
Twin-cylinder Engines—.	
Arrangement of	31, 35
Magneto Setting for	104
System of Working in " V " Type	32–37
Trembler Coil Setting for	115
Valve Mechanism of	33, 35
Two-Speed Gear—	
The Indian	150
Millennium Fit-All	154
" P. & M."	149
Roc	145
"V.S."	143
Two-speed Gears	138, 141, 143
Two-speed Gears, Engine Shaft Types	153
Two-stroke Cycle, The	20
Two-stroke Cycle and Four-stroke, Compared	27
Types of Motor-Cycles, Various	215
Tyre—	
The Continental	243
Dunlop	243, 245
Kempshall	243
Palmer-Cord	243
Peter-Union	244
Shamrock-Excelsior	244
Tyres—	
Care of the	202
for Motor Cycles of varying h.-p.	242
for Side Car Machines	236, 243
Non-Slipping	243

U

NDER-Geared Pulley, The Wanderer	126

Why Stop to Repair Punctures

when the use of Firmax will enable you to reach your journey's end, whatever the distance, even though your Tyres are badly Punctured.

Firmax

is not a Liquid, and does not interfere with patching.

Price per Set for Motor Cycle, 5/-, Post Free.

with full instructions and testimonials, direct from Makers,

Firmax Ltd., Yeovil, England.

Firmax has been granted the ROYAL AUTOMOBILE CLUB Certificate.

P.L. Accumulators.

THESE Accumulators are now well-known, and have given every satisfaction, whe her used for Ignition or Lighting. The cases are of stout celluloid, with only one joint. The Positive Plates are $\frac{1}{4}$-in. thick and have never been known to buckle, and an arrangement of celluloid strips and Separators prevents all rattling. Every Accumulator is guaranteed for one year.

❧ ❧ ❧ ❧

4 Volt. **10/6** 20 Amp.

Other sizes and Prices on Application.

PAISH LANE & COMPY., LIMITED,
250, HIGH HOLBORN, W.C.

Under-Lubricating the Engine 159, 161

V-TYPE—
  Belts and Pulleys 116
  Engines 30–34, 38–41
  Engines, Magnetos for 92, 96, 98
Valveless Engines 20
Valves—
  Action of the 10–13
  Automatic Inlet (A.O.I.V.).. 11, 54
  Automatic Inlet, Adjusting.. 188
  Automatic, Compared with
    Mechanically Operated .. 12
  Automatic, Testing 190
  Grinding in the 60, 185
  Mechanically Operated (M.O.V.)
    11, 53
  Mechanically Operated, Lift
    of 12, 19, 187
  Overhead 12, 34, 38
  Setting of the 14
Valve Springs—
  Appliances for Lifting 186
  Strength of.......... 17, 19, 188
Variable Speed Gears (*see* Gears).
" Veeder " Mileage Recorder, The 258
Vendors, Motor Cycle 212
Vibration, The Question of 165
Voltage—
  Dry Battery 112
  Accumulator 113

" V.S."—
  Adjustable Pulley, The 126
  Motor Bicycle, The 220
  Two-speed Gear and Free
    Engine 143

WALL Motor Tricycle, The .. 240
Wanderer—
  Spring Forks 170, 176
  Twin-cylinder Engine, The.. 41
  Under-geared Engine Pulley 126
Watawata Belt, The 118
Weight of Machine, Avoiding
    Unnecessary 207
Whistles, Exhaust 251
Whittle Belt, The 120
Wipe Contact-breaker 87, 112
Wiring—
  Accumulator Ignition 86
  Armature 89, 93
  Bosch Magneto Ignition 92
  Ignition Coils 86, 114
  Lodge Double-pole Ignition 105
Worm Drive, T.A.C. System of .. 124

XL-ALL Spring Devices 176

ZENITH, Motor Bicycle fitted
  with Gradua Gear 141

H. TAYLOR & Co., *Motor Specialists.*

A WORD WITH YOU.

WE can help you to select the right machine to suit your requirements.

Hold Agencies for all leading makes.

Carry a stock of good reliable second-hand machines for beginners or experts.

Prices from £7 0 0. Exchanges arranged.

Your machine can be equipped from our Showrooms with everything useful.

Our catalogue will help you to select suitable fitments for the machine and waterproof clothing for the rider.

Special tariff rates to our Colonial friends. The London House for Rex machines and spare parts. Repairs a Speciality.

The last word—**Try us!**

21a, Store St. (The Centre for all Motorists) **Tottenham Court Rd.,**
London, W.C.

Telephone: 10957 CENTRAL.   "Telegrams: DYNAMETRO."

There are more patented improvements embodied in 1911

"MONTGOMERY" SIDE CARS

than in all other makes put together. It is these exclusive points which lifts them above all others.

FIT ANY MOTOR CYCLE.

LIST FREE ON REQUEST

The Pick of the Basket.

For the Year "nineteen eleven."

W. MONTGOMERY & CO.,
—— Coventry. ——

London Agents: PHELON & MOORE, Ltd., 12, Mortimer St., W.

ALUMINIUM CASTINGS

For the Model Engineer and other Trades.

COAN CASTS CLEAN CRANK CASES

Castings—Clean and Sound—as supplied for Mr. T. Sopwith's Biplane in the De Forest £4,000 Prize Flight (Cross Channel).

Telephone Nos.
879 Central.
3846 City.

Motor Castings a Speciality.
On Admiralty and War Office Lists.

Telegrams—
"KRANKASES."

R. W. COAN, The Aluminium Foundry,
—— 219, Goswell Road, London, E.C. ——

—— THAT FORK ——

is essential to the perfect equipment of your cycle—for comfort awheel.
—It is the world-famous

—— 'DRUID' ——

—the Spring fork which completely absorbs vibration—eliminates shocks, jars, and bouncing—and enables you to meet every obstacle with a velvety touch.
—Perfect Cycling is an accomplished fact only when this Fork is fitted because it's the *only* fork which makes perfect cycling possible.
—Ask for our Booklet—it will interest you and gives fullest particulars.

**A. DREW & Co., Druid Works,
CONYBERE ST., BIRMINGHAM**

All Makers fit it.

R.H.S.

B & B
THE
HALL-MARK
OF
PERFECTION.

B & B CARBURETTERS.

B & B CARBURETTERS.

DROP US A POSTCARD AND WE WILL SEND YOU, POST FREE, AN ILLUSTRATED BOOKLET CONTAINING HINTS AND TIPS TO MOTOR-CYCLISTS.

BROWN & BARLOW, LTD.
HOLT STREET, BIRMINGHAM.